THE YOUNG ONE

THE YOUNG ONE

THE VIEW FROM THE FRONT LINE

DAVID YOUNG AND **ALAN EVANS**

MAINSTREAM
PUBLISHING

EDINBURGH AND LONDON

To April, Thomas-Rhys, Lewis and Owen,
and my parents and sister

First published in Great Britain in 2001 by
MAINSTREAM PUBLISHING COMPANY
(EDINBURGH) LTD
7 Albany Street
Edinburgh EH1 3UG

ISBN 1 84018 452 3

A catalogue record for this book is available
from the British Library

Typeset in Sabon
Printed and bound in Great Britain by
Butler & Tanner Ltd, Frome and London

ACKNOWLEDGEMENTS

My career as told in this book would never have started in the first place without the support and encouragement of my parents, Robert and Pam Young. As I grew up my sister, Maria, was an ever-present friend with a great interest in Rugby. My wife, April, has been my greatest champion since we first met 15 years ago, always first to say 'well done!' on the good days and always there to gee me up when things were not going smoothly. I am indebted to every one of them for the sacrifices they have made to enable me to continue playing rugby for all these years.

My other great sources of inspiration have been the many teachers and coaches who have given readily of their time to improve me as a player from boyhood. Several of them are mentioned in the pages that follow; but to any whose names I have missed, I can only apologise and plead the effect of packaging down in too many scrums on my memory.

One of the objectives of this book was to set out a record of how all the people mentioned above, whether they be family, friends or coaches, have played their part in everything I have achieved in rugby – and it will also be something for my three sons, Thomas-Rhys, Lewis and Owen, to refer to in years to come when trying to work out why their Dad was away so often when they were youngsters.

Last but not least, I am indebted to Alan Evans for sitting at the other side of the table for many hours, listening to and promoting my reminiscences, and for writing *The Young One*.

David Young
September 2001

CONTENTS

1

CAPTAIN OF WALES

They say that every little boy in my country wants to captain Wales and I was no different from anyone else. The trouble was that I had to wait longer than most. My thirtieth birthday had long since been and gone when the call came and, to be honest, I thought the honour had passed me by. But events can change rapidly in Wales, particularly when it comes to hiring and firing its star rugby players, and that's certainly what happened towards the end of January 2000.

When you've played international rugby one of the first things on your mind every New Year is whether or not you've kept your place in the team for the forthcoming Six Nations' matches. So you can imagine my concern when I was told that Wales coach Graham Henry wanted a quiet word with me. I was travelling back from London on the Cardiff team bus after what had been a very important win in the Heineken Cup match against Harlequins. It had been a desperately tight struggle in the closing stages but we had held on to qualify for the knockout rounds two months later. The journey home was a chance to unwind and relax. The club coach Lynn Howells, who also happened to be Henry's assistant in the Wales set-up, called me down to the front of the bus and said that Graham wanted to see me in his office the next morning. I suddenly stopped and wondered whether there was bad news on the way. Several things went through my mind. Did Graham want to talk about how long I intended to carry on? Worse still, was I about to be dropped?

As things turned out the news was far better than I had dared hope. No sooner had I arrived in his office in Cardiff than Graham Henry said that he wanted to discuss a subject very important and very serious. It concerned the Six Nations' matches about to start in three weeks' time, and Graham was giving serious consideration to his choice of captain. My club-mate Robert Howley had been appointed captain by the previous

Welsh coach, Kevin Bowring, and had continued as captain since Graham had arrived from New Zealand 18 months before. After a shaky start the team had competed well under him. Now Graham wanted to make a change. He felt that Rob's own form was suffering because of the responsibilities of captaincy and he had spoken to him about his concerns. Not surprisingly, perhaps, Rob had disagreed with Graham's opinion but nothing had been settled. Nevertheless he was turning to me and offering me the chance to lead the team.

My first reaction was one of total shock at the offer but not total surprise as Rob had already told me that Graham's concerns about his captaincy was affecting his game. I had captained a few sides in my time but I was not expecting this, least of all now. I told Graham what he was proposing was a great honour but my first thoughts were about Rob. I made no secret of the fact that I was interested but at the same time it was important to me that Graham speak to Rob again. Until the decision was made final I put any idea of being captain out of my head. Graham assured me that he would be seeing Rob before the end of the week and after we had talked again he would make a public announcement.

The meeting had lasted barely half an hour and I drove home to Aberdare to discuss the news with my wife, April, and my father and mother. They were thrilled, as I knew they would be, but the matter was far from settled and I tried as best as I could to put it out of mind. Frankly, I was very aware that from a personal point of view there would be less upset if Rob Howley carried on as captain. April was quick to remind me that I had worked hard all my life and, as far as she and the family were concerned, it was an honour that I deserved. Deep down I knew that she was right. I was 32 and had enjoyed a great career in the game. Leading my country would be a fitting final chapter!

I couldn't ignore the fact that Graham Henry had approached me. Here was a man who had worked with great captains like Sean Fitzpatrick back in Auckland coming to me, not the other way around. I hadn't actively chased the job – but I knew that now that it had been put in front of me there was no turning back. Four days later, far sooner than I had expected, I was back in the same building in Cardiff sitting alongside Graham Henry as he told a packed press conference that I was captain of Wales.

That hadn't been part of the plan at the beginning of the week. It was five o'clock on a dark Friday afternoon and a strange time to be making such an important announcement. But events had gathered a pace of their own. Rob had been told that the captaincy was being given to me and he was keen to issue a press statement of his own. I was training with the Cardiff squad when Graham caught up with me to say that he couldn't wait until after the weekend to make the announcement. In a way this was probably the best thing that could have happened. I had already telephoned Rob for a private chat and I was also feeling very positive myself. The captaincy wouldn't last forever but whilst it did I was determined to enjoy it.

On a personal note, both April and I were extremely anxious that the change in captaincy would not affect our very close friendship with both Rob and his wife, Ceri. She and April had developed a special bond and regularly travelled to away matches together. But it was obvious to everyone that Rob took it very personally and in fact I think for a short while the loss affected his form to a greater extent than the captaincy itself. I would not be honest if I did not say that for a while our relationship as a foursome was put under considerable strain, but happily it did not last that long and Rob continues to give me full support both on and off the field while Ceri and April can often be seen together at Cardiff.

The press conference went well. There's always going to be one tricky question and this time it was short and simple: what did I bring to the captaincy that Rob Howley didn't? I said that Rob had done well as a captain, his record spoke for itself, but we were different personalities and I was looking forward to the challenge. I was also pleased with the initial response from the public. On the Saturday afternoon, Cardiff played a Welsh Cup game against local club Rumney and I was happy to be on the replacements' bench. There was no shortage of well-wishers as I walked along the touch line before and after the match and that meant a lot to me.

I knew that I was ready for the build-up to the first international of the Six Nations' Championship. With France due at the Millennium Stadium a fortnight later we assembled at our training camp in the Vale of Glamorgan and I felt no negative vibes whatsoever from the rest of the Wales squad.

Before we started our first training session Graham Henry spoke to all the players and said that he felt sure that they would give me 100 per cent support. After that it was down to business. The time flew by as we prepared for what we all knew was to be a big test against the French. A series of trial matches was held at St Helens, Swansea in the middle weekend of the build-up and was immediately followed by the announcement of the team. There were no major surprises. Scott Gibbs was injured and the young Newport centre Jason Jones-Hughes took his place. Rob Howley was at scrum-half and Peter Rogers and Garin Jenkins would pack down with me in the front row as they had done throughout the World Cup. My own preparations during the week were very much as they had always been. I have always believed that we should train as we play but as captain I did keep an eye on the body language of the individuals.

My first official engagement as captain was to attend an official dinner with past players – the mentors' dinner! Graham had invited past players such as Gareth Edwards, Barry John, Alan Phillips, Bob Norster and Graham Price to watch the trials and give their views. The dinner was an attempt by Graham to bring past and current players closer together because he felt there was a large barrier between us. I confess to being very sceptical because a lot of these past players worked for the media and made a living out of slagging off current players. They apparently enjoyed it, with the one common theme that we were never going to be as good as them. I understand that if we don't play well we are open to criticism but several of them make the criticism personal, which I feel is unwarranted. They always find fault, win or lose. Whatever Graham and we, as players, did or said, pundits like J.J. Williams, Bobby Windsor and company would not fully support the team. Unfortunately the latest recruit is Gwyn Jones who seems to be fighting hard to be the most negative man in Welsh rugby at the moment. There are, thank God, a few exceptions to the rule, namely Gareth Edwards, Derek Quinnell and a few others who always remain positive and supportive.

Then on the eve of the match itself there was the captain's meeting. This is something special. Only the team and the seven replacements are present, and the captain is very much in charge. My approach was simple. I would tell the team what I expected of them. It was a case of breaking the following day's game into certain areas: how we would attack their weaknesses; how we would play to our strengths. With the French it was vital that we ourselves had a fear factor; we had to be aware, perhaps afraid, of what they could do if we let them run the game. We would have to get on top of them in the scrums and we would have to stop their driving lineouts. And always there was the threat of French flair. We all knew this and my job at the meeting was to reinforce our own attitude and achieve the same mindset by everybody. It was important to me that the players realised that everything I said was coming from the heart as well as the head. But in any Welsh team motivation is rarely a problem. The stakes are too high, as success is almost an expectation with the fans. By the end of the meeting I knew that the boys were ready for the game the next day. Honour and Responsibility are two words that come together when you wear the Welsh shirt. We have the ability to make everyone happy for a few days in the week following a success.

The day of the match couldn't have come soon enough for me. I always have the feeling that I want to get on with it but sometimes with the four o'clock kick-offs the time can drag. Funnily enough that didn't happen this time. In fact, once we got to the stadium I felt rushed in everything I did. In the changing-room I talked to the players about tactics and lineout calls non-stop. Perhaps it was nervous energy, about reassuring myself that everyone's mind was on the job ahead. Suddenly time was running away and, having strapped up, I found myself rushing to get my boots on. The great moment was about to hit me.

That first time when I led Wales out onto the Millennium Stadium will live with me forever. As we came out of the tunnel the roar was immense. The tradition these days is that the team follows behind Shenkin the goat and his goat-major but I would give anything to sprint out like we did in the old days. At least the slow walk had one advantage. It gave me time to take in the huge sense of pride for myself, for April and my three boys, and my parents and all the family. It was a very personal thing.

A few days before the game a letter had been sent to me by a Welsh fan (at least I assume he or she was, but the letter was unsigned) in which the writer said he/she had followed my career very closely and noticed that I never sang the national anthem. This was a serious matter and if I didn't sing it on Saturday when I was captain the press would be notified! What the letter-writer didn't know was that I am a very emotional person. Hundreds of Welsh players over the years have lined up at the old Cardiff Arms Park and now the Millennium Stadium whilst 'Mae Hen Wlad Fy Nhadau' is played and sung. Words cannot describe the feeling but those of us who have experienced it are the privileged few. Some of us sing with a tremendous enthusiasm; others, like Paul Thorburn the first time he was captain, are reduced to tears. I was potentially very much one of the latter camp. I had tried to join in the singing in the past and had soon felt my lips start to quiver.

So on my greatest day I stood there tall and proud and silent, with a lump in my throat as big as a rugby ball, whilst all around me sang. Everything sank in there and then. I looked up into the stand, waved to April, turned and ran to take my position as the whistle blew to start the game. I was captain of Wales. It had been a long road that my family had shared with me every step of the way and for them and me that moment represented the culmination of 15 years of hard work.

2

EARLY DAYS

The road that led to that great moment at the Millennium Stadium may have been a long one, but it had been far from lonely. Every step had been taken with the support of my family. Today I have my wife April and our three sons, Thomas, Lewis and Owen, and from the very beginning there have been my mother and father. My father, Robert Lewis Young, has always been my inspiration. He was a miner who was made redundant from Tower Colliery, in Hirwaun, very early in his working life but that didn't prevent him and my mother, Pamela, instilling in my sister Maria and myself a set of values that I like to think April and I pass on to our own children today.

We were a small but close family. Peter, my father's only brother, married to Judith, represented Boys' Clubs of Wales and is the man in the middle of some first-class rugby. Their two children have close ties with the stadium. Keri is a steward and Sian is a regular supporter of any game of rugby. My mother's sister Maria was married to my Uncle Billy, and Maria and I would spend hours with our cousins Ian and Elizabeth, as there was only a matter of months between us all. The final piece of the jigsaw is my Uncle Joey, my mother's younger brother who taught me how to spin pass. We lived on a large council estate in Penywaun, a few streets away from Uncle Raymond and Auntie Sandra. At their house I would spend a great deal of time playing with my cousin Christopher, who represented Wales at darts. I remember this as a very happy house filled always with the noise of laughter.

I attended Penywaun Primary School where the headmaster was Mr John Jenkins. On our return home in 1996 Mr Jenkins was one of the first to phone and welcome my family back to Wales. It was an area with a lot of unemployment and hardship but where the people were straightforward and friendly.

Even before starting school at the age of three I have vivid memories of toddling along with a rugby ball under my arm heading toward the local rugby pitch with my father. We would spend hours passing or kicking the ball. I cannot remember getting tired or bored and my father would end up carrying me screaming back home for the pre-bedtime bath before supper.

Every Saturday afternoon my father would play prop for Aberaman. I always watched from the sideline and became known as the toddler in the duffle coat and wellies. After the game we would return to the club for the after-match discussions and catch up on the football and rugby results on *Grandstand*. I would sit alongside him listening to every word. The only time the room ever went quiet was when *Tom and Jerry* appeared on the television; suddenly these craggy-faced men were gazing at the screen with child-like smiles. It is a memory that will always stay with me. It was one of these men, Mansel Swales, who said continually that I would captain Wales one day; unfortunately he died in a car accident before it happened. I like to think that I never missed a game played by my father and later he certainly never failed to turn up to watch me.

As the years passed I started to play mini-rugby with Hirwaun and Aberaman in order to satisfy my increasing appetite for the game and to ease the persistent nagging of my parents. At the age of five or six I won a Player of the Tournament award for Hirwaun under-nines, something which would not happen today as sensible rules have been introduced to protect youngsters from injury.

In the junior school years I had the best of both worlds. Whilst my father encouraged and supported me out of school, I was also lucky enough to have a sport-mad class teacher, Leighton Rees. Mr Rees was instrumental in changing school rules. He made it possible for boys to play school rugby and football from Standard 3 instead of Standard 4. He thought that if someone was good enough they were old enough. I remember Mr Rees playing football and rugby at break time, spending most of his dinner hour and hours after school improving players' skills and, although I was only in Standard 3, I was always invited to join in.

At this age one player who stood out and who I looked up to was Paul Williams. Moran, as he was known, was a strong left-footer who could do things with a football that most kids could only dream of at that age. He was also a very good rugby player. I still find it hard to believe that he did not find his way into professional football because I am sure that there are professional footballers with less talent than Paul had. I suppose that he did not have the little bit of luck we all need.

Mr Rees built up a tremendous reputation for the school in sport in the Cynon Valley and we became the team everyone aspired to beat. They, myself included, although I was a year younger than the rest, went on to win all major school tournaments and supplied the bulk of players for the Cynon Valley rugby and soccer under-11s. So by the time I was in Standard 3 there I was, already bitten by the rugby bug.

The Cynon Valley Schools Rugby team under coach Dave Pritchard reached the D.C. Thomas Cup final against Bridgend at the Brewery Field. We lost narrowly and it was a disappointing end to the season as we completed one of the most successful runs in the team's history. We were fortunate as a team to have Dave as our coach. No one could doubt his commitment to the area. He could regularly be seen transporting children playing for a particular team of his to competitions all over the place. At these tournaments he would ensure they had food and drink at his own expense, as their parents were often unemployed. Mountain Ash where he taught, within the Cynon Valley, was and still is one of the most deprived areas in Wales.

The following year was my last year in junior school. All my team mates from school rugby and football had progressed to the comprehensive schools so it was inevitable that I would have my first taste of captaincy. I like to think that it was not only because of my size but also my ability. I captained Penywaun and Cynon Valley football and rugby teams for that year. I was also selected to play for East Wales under-11s against West Wales, which was the highest honour achievable in rugby at that age.

Another pupil of Mr Rees and a friend of mine was Neil Edwards, someone who had that little bit of luck to go with his immense talent as a goalkeeper. He was also a neighbour of mine, although younger, and, after a successful schools career where he gained caps at all levels, went on to represent Leeds and Stockport. He is currently at Rochdale. I would like to think that I contributed to his success after all the shots I fired at him after school against our neighbour's wall. Eddie, Neil's dad, was probably one of the first people I ever passed a ball to. Although I was bigger, older and kicked with all my strength, Neil was always up to the save. Neil, also, could always rely on the total support of his parents, Neta and Eddie.

Mr Rees used my natural interest in sport to develop other skills. I was a bit of a reluctant reader but he encouraged me by bringing in rugby and football books that he knew I would throw myself into. He was right and my reading improved, if not as quickly as my progress in the games lessons. I became school captain in both rugby and soccer. He will forgive me for saying this — he has only one fault; he is a Scarlet through and through and he says he can't understand how I never played for them.

My mother, on the other hand, always stayed in the background. She worked at a local factory as a line manager and she only returned to work when she was sure that Maria and I were capable of looking after ourselves. She was known affectionately as 'Pwm' and when the need arose she was quick to defend us. Being big for my age had its disadvantages as well as pluses. I remember one occasion when Mr Jenkins, the headmaster, sent for my mother because her big boy had punched a 'little' boy. The fact was that this little boy along with several others had been, over the previous couple of months, taunting me. I had gone home on several occasions with cuts and bruises but because I was so much bigger than the rest of my class I would not retaliate. My parents' words would echo in my ears 'Don't you go hitting anyone smaller than yourself.' Until one day they pushed me too far and I gave the 'little boy' a bit of a clip. I suppose it was a fair cop but as my mother was quick to point out to Mr Jenkins no discussion had taken place between them regarding the cuts and bruises I had sustained. She said that there comes a time when you have to stand up for yourself and she felt I had been more than tolerant.

One thing that upsets my mother, and now April as well, is when people call me 'Dai'. 'His name is David,' they say. They find it even more annoying if people use Dai when they do not know me personally. To be honest, I get a bit confused myself. I was nearly ten before I realised that my name was David Young and not 'Daiyoung' because the Christian and surnames seemed to roll off the tongue as one name.

I was, and still am, very close to my sister. Maria is eleven months younger than me but braver than I was. She was always first down the stairs on Christmas Day, not by choice but because I was too chicken to go and explore what was waiting for us. On one occasion I had a new bike and came across a steep hill. Maria got off her bike, and pushed her big brother to the top before going back for hers. As we grew up she was never far from the rugby action in our house. I always say that she's the best loose-head in the business because whenever my father wanted to demonstrate a scrummaging technique to the budding tight-head of a son, it was always Maria who packed down. In every sense of the word she has been supportive to me and she is still a sister in a million.

I like to think that by the time I moved on to Aberdare Boys Comprehensive School, from Penywaun Junior School, I had the attitude I still have today, which is that education is very important and that it is a great aid to setting yourself up in a career. That is what our parents had taught both Maria and me. Looking back over 20 years I can't honestly remember what I was like as a pupil but as an 11-year-old I was, of course, sport-mad. I enjoyed school because there was plenty of sport and I was good at most of it. At the senior school the rugby, cricket, soccer and athletics teams all tended to have the same boys playing for them and it suited me down to the ground. But as much as I liked soccer, it still came second to rugby. Where Leighton Rees had been a great help at the junior school, I now came across another inspiring teacher in Kenneth Morgan; and when I was chosen to play for the district side, Cynon Valley Schools, in the premier under-15s competition, the Dewar Shield, the coach was again Dave Pritchard.

Mr Rees, Mr Morgan and Mr Pritchard have all played an important part in furthering my ambitions and I remain grateful to them to this day.

The major influence, though, remained my father. He took me to all the training sessions as my career developed and he would sit for hours in any weather that was thrown at him until the last ball was kicked or passed. He thought nothing of waiting for me to shower and then in the car on the way home he would discuss the session and talk about technique or a tradesman's trick that he thought would contribute towards my development as a prop. He spoke from experience as he had played in the position for Aberaman Rugby Club for more than 25 years. It was from him that I had my first lessons in feet and arm positions in the scrum.

It was also an advantage to be part of a good school team and it was no coincidence that when the great day came and I was chosen to captain Wales at under-15 level, two others from the school were in the team with me. Huw Jones was a quick and big number 8 and Nick Davies a flanker who later, in senior rugby, was to play the odd game for Swansea and several seasons for South Wales Police. Another Aberdare Comprehensive School pupil who was to make his mark at Cardiff and with Wales was David Evans. He was at this time making progress through the ranks playing at either outside-half or full-back, and played for Wales under-16s at the same time as we three were playing for Wales under-15s. David was an annoying sportsman who seemed to be good at everything he did. Throughout our school years we played a lot of rugby and football together where David was always the leading light. He was a real character both on and off the field with always a joke to share with you and always a smile on his face.

I was lucky enough to win three caps at under-15 level and the following year played for the under-16s against England. The chairman of selectors told me that although I had previous experience as captain he did not see how a prop could captain an international team. Karl Gupwell, a centre, was named captain for the first time.

The school years flew by and I left when I was 16, determined to reach the top in rugby and equally determined to secure my future with a decent occupation. This was a theme that continued, and when it came to getting a good job it became obvious that it was not going to be all plain sailing.

But back in 1983 the signs were good. No sooner had I left school than I went to work for a builders' merchants, Magnet & Southerns, as a trainee manager. That sounds very grand and, yes, it was a foot on the ladder that I hoped would lead to greater things. The manager at the firm was John Moss and I was paid £35 a week. Nearly 20 years ago that was a good wage. I was still living at home and my only expenditure was the kit I needed for my rugby and a few drinks on a Saturday night.

By now I was playing for Aberaman Youth and we were kept in line by an excellent committee. David Picton at the helm with his right hand men Ray Stacey, Elwyn Gay and Glyn Chivers. The Four Musketeers worked tirelessly to make sure that we had everything we needed for a game but more importantly that we enjoyed ourselves at the same time. They were always eager to be the post-match entertainment on the team bus home. We were a team made up of locals and, importantly, we were all friends.

We had success on the field and I believe we were one of the most successful youth teams in the history of Aberaman. The coach was Morton Jones, an ex-hooker, who was renowned in the valleys. He was a rugby fanatic and a great motivator. He knew forward play inside out. Morton was someone to be respected but also someone who could be learned from. Phil Rees, another quietly spoken teacher, was the backs' coach. He was a deep thinker about the game and always turned up at training with a new move or tactic to confuse the opposition. These two combined to make a formidable coaching team. The game was always followed by the traditional relaxation. That was fine by me but I also remained very dedicated.

During my second season of youth rugby I was invited to play for the Cardiff Youth side and for the first half of that season I did so. There were a few players there like Mike Parry who I already knew from the Wales Schools' team of a couple of years before. I finished work at 5.30 p.m. weekdays and 12.30 p.m. on a Saturday so the two hours spent travelling twice a week for training, as well as playing, became too much. By the time Christmas came I had returned to Aberaman, though the fact that other clubs were taking an interest in me certainly fuelled my ambition. I had established a bit of a reputation in youth rugby as a technically good prop who was also mobile and scored a few tries. I eventually got into the Mid-District team and then played in a final trial for Wales.

It was another big moment for me when I played for Wales Youth in 1985. I was still only 17 and if all went well I could look forward to a couple of seasons in the side before I stepped up to senior rugby, but I soon realised I had much to learn. The coach was Ron Waldron, a man for whom I quickly came to have a huge respect. He had been through the mill as a prop forward himself and had made a little bit of history when he was chosen for his first senior cap for Wales against Ireland in Dublin only for the match to be postponed. When the game was eventually played six months later he was left out and he had to wait three long years before he made his international debut at the age of 31. Ron was the first real disciplinarian I came across who I would liken to a drill sergeant. He would bark out orders and placed huge emphasis on fitness, teamwork and being mentally tough but with a real understanding for game plan awareness. He also knew the importance of a sense of humour, often using it to relieve pain and suffering.

Prior to the squad announcement for a tour to Canada, I had already played one game for Neath against the Crawshays XV and two for Swansea. There had been one or two discussions between Ron and myself when he said that he would like me to join Neath on a permanent basis but I don't know what he thought after I took part in one of the club's legendary runs to the top of a dam. I can still see now the wiry figure of their first team prop Brian Williams way ahead of me as he disappeared over the horizon. Williams was a farmer from Cardiganshire and one of the true hard men of rugby. Funnily enough I won my senior cap before him and when I left union to play rugby league he very shortly afterwards came into the Wales team at loose-head with his club-mate Jeremy Pugh filling my position at tight-head.

After my first few training sessions with Ron I was beginning to think that I might also have to wait until I was in my thirties before I would be ready for top honours. He introduced me to a level of training that I found totally new. At one point he took the youth touring squad down to his home club of Neath to join in their pre-season preparation. I was 19 and about to leave the youth ranks but first I was to lead the Wales Youth team on the Canadian tour. The team seemed to be shaping up nicely. I was captain in my second season and had Leighton Gerrard and Leyton Phillips alongside me in the front row and a future senior cap Andy Allen packing down behind us at lock. There were also two big pals of mine in the side; Richard Webster and Anthony Clement. Both Webby and Clem were to play important roles in my changing fortunes over the next three or four years.

Anthony Clement was by far the most accomplished outside-half I had played with to date. He possessed all the skills, pace and game awareness that was sure to make him a class act in senior rugby. For an average sized outside-half he had stacks of guts, he was powerful and very hard to stop; but the big thing that stood out was his ability to kick the ball. He could kick out of hand without much effort from one 22 to the other, which made him the forwards' dream. He was also a great goal kicker with a range of 50 to 60 metres. His one fault was his lack of confidence in his own ability. He would shy away from taking penalties and conversions and I remember making him take kicks for goals when he was reluctant to do so, kicks he slotted over with great ease. My strongest memory of playing youth rugby with Clem was telling him to have a crack at a drop goal when he had the opportunity. To my amazement he ended up dropping two goals from inside his own half. I have yet to see any drop goal from such a distance out.

So we thought we were a good team and it was no secret that we were considered the best Welsh Youth side for several years. That was until we went to Le Teste in the south of France and were hammered by 40 points. We came up against a French side that played a totally different physical game from what we were used to. We soon learned that we couldn't take any liberties. When Webby was just a little bit late with his tackle on the French fly-half all hell broke loose and there was a free-for-all. We won about 20 per cent of the possession in the game and in a way did well to limit them to five tries against one of our own.

It was a much more comfortable experience to go to Canada in the late summer of 1986. After our hard build-up, not least that training camp down at Neath, most of the games were quite easy until we got to Vancouver to play British Columbia. They were known as the premier side in Canada and were prepared to do anything to live up to their reputation. They were very physical off the ball but they had quality players including 11 of the Canada team that was due to play us a week later. It was again a bit of a bloodbath but we soaked up the pressure and won the match 16–13. Unfortunately this game and the intensity of the training throughout the tour took its toll on the team and we lost the test the following week, which was a disappointing note on which to end what had been a successful tour.

The evening following the test, when Ron and I were quietly reflecting on events, he spoke to me about joining Neath. I told him that I had already made up my mind to join Swansea. Clem and Webby were also joining them which would make things a lot easier; and Stuart Evans who was the incumbent Welsh prop had in any case just returned to Neath. Although I could learn from Stuart I felt that my games would be limited. Swansea were desperate for tight-head and it made more sense to go there. Ron's response was, 'I hope you spew over your blazer tonight.' He assured me, however, that if I should ever change my mind I would be always welcome at Neath.

Most of the squad touring Canada had already played a few senior games at the tail end of the previous season and were already working, but as soon as we arrived home we would be looking for new clubs on a more permanent basis. That certainly applied to me. Like Webby and Clem I had already played a couple of games for Swansea and it never occurred to me that it would be anything more than a formality for me to resume my contact with the All Whites on my return. How wrong I was!

I quickly discovered that the powers-that-be at Aberaman Rugby Club were not prepared to sanction my transfer to Swansea. Aberaman chairman Humphrey Evans quoted a long-standing tradition, in his eyes at least, that a youth player should play a season of senior rugby for the club that had developed him. He also argued that I would be a better player in the long run if I eased my way into the first-class scene after playing for Aberaman. I couldn't agree with him and neither could my father. Five months before, in one of my 'permit' games for Swansea, I had packed down against the famous Cardiff front-row of Jeff Whitefoot,

Alan Phillips and Ian Eidman and I had held my own. I had also shown some mobility around the park – I can even remember chasing Cardiff's outstanding half-back Gareth Davies and catching him behind his own goal line.

Experiences like that had served only to further strengthen my resolve and my ambition. I had come back from Canada buzzing. I had led a team brimful with players of my own age whose future in first-class rugby had already been sealed. Now I was being told that I wasn't ready for the big step up and my immediate future lay with Aberaman.

This was not a situation I was comfortable with. Aberaman had been good to me and, I liked to think, I had also served them well. I was not turning my back on the area because I would continue to live there and one day, I hoped, would put something back into local rugby through coaching. That, by the way, is something that did happen ten years later when I returned from my travels and combined my playing career for Cardiff with coaching Abercynon and Aberdare (as Aberaman had by then become). Back in 1986, however, there was only one man who could sort out the threatened deadlock – my father. After a quarter of a century at the local club he was the best man to open doors and change minds. Sure enough he went to the committee and Humphrey Evans, to his great credit, announced with regret that David Young would be transferred to Swansea Rugby Club. It was made clear though that they thought that I would spend most of my time on the bench for Swansea and probably come running back with my tail between my legs and plenty of splinters in my bum.

A great adventure was about to begin.

3

INTO SENIOR RUGBY

There were several good reasons for my wanting to go to Swansea in 1986. I was flattered that other clubs had shown an interest, particularly Neath with whom I had trained and for whom I had also played a game against Crawshays XV. Cardiff had also kept in touch after my appearances for their youth side. But Swansea were in pole position because I had finished the previous season with them on permit and there was an assumption that they had been a springboard for a full transfer. They also had a vacancy at tight-head prop after Keith Colclough had moved across to loose-head when their British Lion Clive Williams had retired.

A vacancy was created that if all went well, I felt sure I could fill. And as always my father played a part. He had sorted out the problems at Aberaman and at Swansea he was very friendly with John 'the pop' Williams. John had been at St Helen's for two or three years doing all the unspectacular work in the second row of the pack and he had no doubt that Swansea was the club for me. He looked after me from day one. I did not have a reliable car at the time so every training night John would pick me up from work and we would travel together to St Helen's for training.

The final ingredient was added when the Swansea committee promised to find me another job. The decision was finalised in my mind. I still worked at Magnet & Southerns but now there was the prospect of better opportunities opening up for me. To play rugby and have good career prospects were always my priorities.

With all the transfer problems well and truly behind me I arrived at Swansea full of enthusiasm and looking forward to learning a lot and establishing a first team place. It was a good time to arrive there. The coach was Jeff Herdman, an ex-hooker who had been good enough to play for the Barbarians and Wales 'B' and he knew the ins and outs of front-row play. There was also a nucleus of great club players especially the Moriarty brothers, Richard and Paul. Dickie was the older of the two and went on to captain Wales. Over the years he picked up a reputation of being, to put it politely, an abrasive player but no one could ever accuse him of dodging the heat of battle. When he went onto the field for Swansea he had a job to do and he certainly did it. He was also an incredibly skilful forward but, more than anything, he was a Swansea 'Jack' through and through. Most important of all for a young player like myself he was totally supportive as I found my feet in my new surroundings.

So was his brother Paul – he was three years older than me but for the next decade or so our paths in rugby were to cross regularly. He had already played for Wales when I joined Swansea and little did I realise that within a very short space of time he and I would be playing in the same international pack. Muzzy was a very skilful player with a ball in hand or at his feet. Apparently he was an excellent soccer player in school. One of Paul's first acts at every training session was to practise his kicking out of hand or place kicking and he was often engaged in kicking competitions with more recognised goal-kickers. He is a hard man on the field and we soon struck up a great friendship off it. I will always remember Paul's generosity – after my first cap against England in Brisbane he came over to me in the dressing-room following the final whistle and gave me his jersey. He knew that I would not want to swap my first senior Welsh jersey so gave me his to exchange with Paul Rendall. But although we are great friends we don't see eye to eye on everything. The great thing I admire about him is that he always says that he would never play rugby union for any club other than Swansea – and he's never slow to remind me that he could not imagine any circumstances under which he would play for Cardiff! He also says that he considers me to be a Swansea Jack deep down as he feels I am not like the rest of those Cardiff city slickers!

The characters and the influences at Swansea didn't stop with the Moriarty's. As I said, Keith Colclough had done me a huge favour by switching to loose-head. He had also played for Wales at schools and youth levels – though long before I did, I hasten to add – and he was a very good prop. 'Cloughie' taught me a lot and I'm sure that if he had been a bit bigger he would have won a few senior caps. Years later he was to move back to the other side of the scrum and at the age of 35 gave a young Wallaby prop, who had been flown over to join their tour, a right going-over as Swansea won a famous victory over the tourists.

There were plenty of other experienced heads in the pack with the English international Maurice Colclough in the second row. Maurice taught me how to lift at the lineout but disguise it, so that it would not be noticed by the officials (this was in the days prior to legal lifting). He had been working together with Fran Cotton on this 'trick' within the England set-up. Also there was Mark Davies, known to all as 'Carcass'. on the flank Mark later became the Wales team physiotherapist. In the backs stood Dai Richards, a real character who was coming to the end of his playing career but was still the life and soul of the team. 'Dennis the Menace' was not someone you wanted to share a room with, as his pranks were legendary. Lighting newspapers whilst they were being read by unsuspecting team-mates was one of the more harmless of his party pieces and anything could happen when Dennis was in full flow on away trips. These days he is in charge of the Welsh Students teams and the mind boggles at how Dennis keeps a straight face if and when he gives them pep talks on the need for self-discipline and good behaviour.

The other great thing for me about being at Swansea at that particular time was that, as I have said, two of my best friends, Richard Webster and Anthony Clement, were also there. We had progressed through the youth ranks together and the welcome that all three of us received only strengthened the feeling that I had made the right move. Another one of the younger brigade, and partnering Clem at half-back, was the 21-year-old Robert Jones. He had already broken into the Wales team the previous season. In other words the team had a good mix of experience and youth and in those days before league rugby was introduced we performed well in the only competition that mattered, the Schweppes Cup.

We sailed through the early rounds and beat Newbridge in the semi-final. As luck would have it our opponents in the Cup final at the National Stadium were Cardiff and I found myself in opposition to the same all-international front row that the season before I had played against on permit. A year down the road taking on Whitefoot, Phillips and Eidman hadn't got any easier. 'Thumper' Phillips was still calling the shots – and doing all the talking. Jeff Whitefoot was still an outstanding loose-head – I could only learn from scrummaging against him but again I came out of it in one piece. I did, however, leave the field at the end of the game with an imprint of highly polished Adidas boots on the back of my head, compliments of Messrs Whitefoot and Norster. Cardiff had decided to play the game 'tight' and win it through their pack, but we more than held our own up front and took the match into extra time. The only blot on the day was when we eventually lost the game through a late dropped goal by Mike Rayer.

The personal disappointment at the end of my first senior season didn't last long, however, because something even more exciting was in the pipeline. Plans had been made for Webby and me to go to Australia for the summer where we could work and play rugby. The Northern Suburbs club of Canberra had toured the UK and played Swansea the season before and one of our committee men, Roger Blyth, had kept in touch with them. Out of that contact had come the suggestion that two young players from Swansea would benefit from a summer playing rugby in a totally different environment. As the discussions advanced they reached the stage where my name and also Richard Webster's were put forward.

The chance to go out there was too good to turn down. There was no financial incentive because we would both be expected to pay our way. We would be working five days a week in Canberra as well as playing rugby at the weekends. It was obviously a chance for us to widen our experience and, most important of all, come back as better players. The downside, for me at least, was that I would have to give up my job at Magnet & Southerns and that would be difficult, not least because security was still something that was always in my mind. On the other hand, Swansea were still promising to find me a job and they reassured me that by the time I returned home in August all the necessary arrangements would have been made. So really there was no choice at all.

There was one hiccup. The week before we were due to travel someone realised that neither Richard nor I had a visa – a necessary requirement for any visit to Australia. We travelled with Roger Blyth to London and after driving through some horrendous traffic arrived at Passport House with 20 minutes to spare. They were very helpful and we were able to return to Wales ready for our journey. With Webby at my side we set off for Australia on the Monday after the Cup final. Neither of us had any idea that when we returned almost four months later it would be as fully-fledged Welsh internationals.

As arranged beforehand, a flat in Canberra was waiting for us to live in and we were quite happy with that. For the first ten days or so we settled in, finding our way around and being introduced to various people involved with the Northern Suburbs club. One of them was their chairman, Ron. He was a butcher so we never went short of good meat, but we did feel that we had been provided only with the basic necessities. After sorting out things like TV, telephone etc., however, we noticed a marked change in the club's attitude towards us. We had played a few games for them by then and we felt that once they appreciated our commitment to their cause they became more eager to help. One of the club's players even lent us his car.

What didn't go quite so smoothly were the efforts to find us jobs so that we could have money in our pockets. Webby is a bricklayer by trade, and they eventually found him work on a building site. He wasn't exactly over the moon to discover that he was paid on a piece work basis and was expected to work from 7 a.m. to 4 p.m. After three days Richard Webster and the Australian bricklaying industry went their separate ways.

I fared a little better, working for two weeks as a plumber's mate on very modest wages. I also worked as a gardener but unfortunately I do not make friends easily with funnel-web spiders and the like. For the remainder of my time I worked at the Parliament building in Canberra, moving fire doors around. Unfortunately my sense of direction is not very good and despite a map of the building to help me I became the bane of the carpenters' lives because the doors somehow were never in the right place. I think they only persisted with me because I was able to lift those incredibly heavy doors.

But in the land of Oz there is always the weekend. We both had to admit that the Aussie way of life was different from anything we had experienced back home. Everything was geared towards sport and leisure and that suited us down to the ground. It soon became obvious that the weekend started promptly at lunchtime every Friday and from then on relaxation and enjoyment was the word. There was certainly no blazer-and-tie formality at the rugby club. I remember the two of us going to our first function there to find a bloke vomiting at the top of the stairs and at the bottom of them another bloke slumped in the corner. Just like back home you might say, but there was far more to their way of life than that. There was also the intense commitment that they gave to their sport and, more than anything, winning and winning well was always the aim.

We were fortunate to be with a good bunch of lads who were eager to do well. Souths and Queenbien were normally the two teams fighting for the top spot in the Canberra League with Norths not faring much better than middle table through previous seasons. It was unusual for teams to bring in overseas players so Norths attracted quite a lot of attention when they imported two young Welsh players. The only previous Welsh international was Robert Ackerman. It was a bit disconcerting when one official in Canberra said to me, 'We hope you're not like Ackerman'! I was to find out several years later exactly what they meant. Robert Ackerman formerly of Newport, Wales and later Whitehaven and Leeds RLFC was in the distant future to be my best man. (One player who originated from Canberra and later went on to play international rugby for Australia was David Campese.)

Remember that back in Wales in 1987 we had no experience of clubs chasing league points week after week – it would be another three years before they were established at home. The training was not what we were used to at Swansea, but it should be remembered that Swansea were well established. Norths were a relatively new team, in an area that was fighting to become a recognised rugby union area, in a country where rugby league is the more popular sport. It soon became apparent that the players and staff at Norths would be learning more from us than we from them.

In the area was the newly built Australian Institute of Sport, and our first team coach, Mark McGarry, was the head groundsman. With his help we gained access to the Institute's incredible facilities and we were given expert advice with our weight-training programmes. This was in 1987; it was only in 2001 that UWIC in Cardiff was given its status as a national training facility.

The team training, on the other hand, was done on the rugby oval in the middle of nowhere and when it came to the real game on the Saturday afternoon nothing was held back. It was very physical and for newcomers like ourselves we were natural targets for two or three 'blues', which you could loosely translate as unprovoked violence, every game. And it helped to toughen us up. Strictly speaking Webby and I were a better class of player than our team mates – in fact you could say that the two of us *were* their pack, but as the weeks went by, as our own standards improved, so did those of the players around us.

Then, out of the blue, came the phone call that would see a dream come true sooner than I could have dared hope. I was called up to play for Wales. The circumstances surrounding this marvellous news were probably unique. The first-ever World Cup tournament was taking place in New Zealand and Australia and by today's standards it was a pretty low-key affair. The governing bodies and committee-men spread out around the world had agonised for years over whether or not our amateur game needed such a competition but, apparently with doubt still in their minds, they had given it the green light. There were no qualifying rounds, just 16 teams invited to compete at various venues spread across the two countries.

Wales were based in New Zealand for their three pool matches and Webby and I had followed their progress with a lot of interest, even though in Canberra the television and newspaper coverage wasn't great. Both of us had been involved in the pre-tournament preparation that had taken place in Wales at the end of our domestic season. The Welsh Rugby Union had picked not one but three squads for the World Cup and, at 19 years old, I was more than a little pleased to be pencilled in for the third squad. At that stage of my career it was a huge boost to my confidence.

They and the senior players certainly noticed me at the first training session I attended, but not for any rugby reason. I was very nervous driving to that session, and I had borrowed my father's car. Turning into the stadium and driving down the ramp by Cardiff Rugby Club my stomach was churning. I had turned left to park under the stand when I heard an almighty crack, and I looked in my mirror to see Jonathan and Phil Davies in hysterics. I had parked on the gatepost of the main security gates. It needed both of them to help me bump the car off. This event caused a long tail-back of seasoned internationals who were waiting to drive in and park themselves. Seeing them leave their cars to come and watch the fun was not my preferred choice of making a first impression on these established stars of Welsh rugby. When the training session finally got under way I was still worrying about how I could explain the damage to my father when I arrived home. The story I eventually dreamt up was that Jeremy Pugh had caused me to swerve when he was speeding away from training. So 15 years on Dad and Jeremy might still want to have a chat with me.

Ahead of me in the pecking order were the first choices, Stuart Evans and the Cardiff pair of Ian Eidman and Steve, or 'Wally', Blackmore. I had no quibbles with that. Evans had made a big reputation for himself as a scrummager and I realised that if I was going to break into the Welsh team in the next two or three years I would have to better the high standards he had set.

Little did I know that fate would take a hand to help me and also that Stuart would be heading north to play league much sooner than anyone had anticipated. More immediately, though, I heard that he had fractured his right foot in the second game and had been flown home. The implications of that didn't register because Blackmore was with the squad and I assumed Eidman was on stand-by to fly out. I was more concerned with following the fortunes of the team – they were certainly doing well and having won all three pool games they had qualified for the knock-out stages of the competition.

The first news I had that I was going to be directly involved was when April called from Aberdare. Apparently a reporter with the BBC in Cardiff had contacted my parents to say that I was about to be drafted into the Welsh squad. I hardly had time to think about this before I received the official call myself telling me to fly up to Brisbane where Wales would be playing their quarter-final against England in three days' time. Suddenly I understood the meaning of that old saying about feet never touching the ground. Webby was almost as delighted as I was and I left Canberra still thinking that I was being sent for as a precaution in case something should happen to Wally Blackmore.

As things turned out I reached Brisbane before the official party who were flying over from Auckland. I checked into the team's hotel still wondering what would happen next in that 'mad' week. When the team arrived a few hours later I couldn't have been made more welcome. The first players I saw were Jonathan Davies and Paul Moriarty and they were enthusiastic about my joining them. I could sense the excitement in the entire squad because the tournament had gone well for them so far and who better to play in the quarter-final than England! They seemed a happy party but there was no time for sitting around and patting each other on the back. There would be two training sessions the next day.

I also had to be kitted out in a team uniform. The manager was one of the great characters of rugby, Clive Rowlands. I had known Clive when I had played with his son Dewi for Wales Youth. Clive lives and breathes the game. He must hold some sort of record in that he captained Wales in every one of his 13 internationals in the 1960s, then coached the side during the glory days of the early 1970s, and went on every one of the national team's first six tours overseas. He was ideally suited to be manager at the World Cup and it wasn't likely that much would throw him off his stride.

He was on top form when I met him and it was typical of Clive to say, 'You may or may not be any good but you must look the part – you are now a member of the Wales squad!' So off I went with the WRU secretary Ray Williams to be kitted out with the obligatory blazer and tie.

Clive had even more of a surprise in store for me later in the day when he announced the team to play England. As I say I had touched down in Brisbane expecting to be on standby for the big match but as I sat there listening, there was no Wally Blackmore in the team but there was David Young. This was what you might call a bit of a shock, not to mention a cause for sheer elation. All that my father and I had worked towards for all those years had suddenly come to fruition on the other side of the world.

The joy was shared back home. Aberaman's chairman Humphrey Evans visited my parents and offered, on behalf of the club, to pay for my father to fly to Brisbane to watch the quarter-final against England. He is a very private man, however, and not a great traveller, and I think he felt the emotion of the occasion would have been too much. He decided that he would prefer to watch the game at home.

I understood his feelings completely. For myself I was a bit apprehensive about the match ahead as I would be up against Paul Rendall, an experienced loose-head who had come into international rugby comparatively late in his career but who was considered a particularly awkward bloke to scrummage against. As was often the case in those days when England were, to say the least, unsuccessful at the top level, the London-based press were still talking them up and making them favourites to go through to a semi-final. We couldn't understand that at all and as the match drew nearer we were quietly confident.

Packing down with me in the front row would be Alan Phillips and Anthony Buchanan and I knew I would be well looked after. 'Thumper' Phillips was the perfect hooker and a real character. He had seen it all in his time and had been a Lion in South Africa seven years before. He had faded out of the test scene for five years and had been called out to join the squad when Billy James had cried off. The years in the international wilderness hadn't dimmed his enthusiasm. He is a great talker who you could guarantee would get under the skin of the opposition, but the pre-match chat he had with me was of a much quieter variety. He took me to one side, put his arm around me and calmly convinced me that he was looking forward to playing with me as we took England apart. That made me feel much better.

There was no shortage of advice, also, from Thumper's Cardiff team mate Jeff Whitefoot. He was a fearsome scrummager who had gone out to the World Cup as first-choice loose-head but after playing in all the pool matches an injury had sidelined him. He said that all I could do was give it my best and he was sure my best was good enough.

One way or another I had all the support I could possibly have asked for and by the time the match started I was not particularly nervous. Over the years I never had been and once everything was under way I was fine. I had gone onto the pitch with those two words from years before ringing in my ears: Honour and Responsibility. My father wasn't there; neither were my mother, my sister or April, but I knew everyone would be spiritually with me. I started the game with ten stitches in a cut on my forehead. It opened almost immediately and blood flowed continuously down my face. It was not painful but it certainly looked impressive. The game was by no means easy. It was hard and it was physical and, looking back, it's right what they say about your first international being over before you know it. I won't pretend that I wasn't getting tired in the final stages, though, and then it was a case of gritting my teeth and getting on with it. Then I saw that England were preparing to replace Rendall and on the touch-line they had Gareth Chilcott warming up. It would be an interesting experience, to say the least, to have Coochie joining Brian Moore in their front row but it hardly mattered because we were in control of a tight game. In the end we won by three tries to nothing and there was no arguing with that.

When we returned to our changing-room there was a lot of celebration and a sense of satisfaction that it had been a job well done. There was a spring in our step for the days that followed but at the back of our minds was the fact that, although we were now in the semi-final of the World Cup, we were now on course to face the favourites, New Zealand.

That match, of course, turned out to be very different. The All Blacks were destined to go on to be the first world champions and they were in no mood to hang around against us. They swept us away with two tries in the first ten minutes and finished up with eight in a 49–6 hammering. On a personal note, playing against Paul Rendall and the England front row was one thing; Steve McDowell, Sean Fitzpatrick and John Drake was something else altogether. I have no doubt that McDowell is the best prop I have ever come up against and Fitzpatrick was notoriously abrasive, yet I felt comfortable against them. We had made a change at hooker with Alan Phillips giving way to his Neath namesake, Kevin. He was a wiry customer who knew how to look after himself and as a unit we held our own. The early scrums went well. I had decided to pack as low as possible and this, apart from anything else, would help stop the All Blacks' drive. They took exception to this and what followed for the next hour or so was no garden party. But I wouldn't relent and would like to think I earned a grudging respect from Steve McDowell. Two weeks before I had been playing club rugby in Canberra and now I had survived against one of the best teams the modern game had seen.

I finished the game with a black eye and my nose half-way to the side of my face but it was an experience from which I could only benefit. It was a timely reminder that I was far from the finished article and the Wales camp as a whole was hugely disappointed. In the cold light of the next day we could reflect that we had come up against an aggressive, mobile and ball-in-hand style of rugby that had rarely been seen before. Clive Rowlands had faced up to the press with a comment that would come back to haunt Welsh rugby when, in response to a question about where we went from here, he came up with the immortal words, 'We'll have to go back to beating England every year . . .'

In fact, where we went next was back across the Tasman Sea to play a third and fourth place match against Australia. No one quite knew what to make of this. The Wallabies had been expected to play the All Blacks in the final the following Saturday. Instead they had been turfed out in front of their own crowd in Sydney after an injury-time try by Serge Blanco of France. How would they approach what many were already calling a meaningless match against Wales? My limited contact with the Aussie mentality in Canberra left me in no doubt that if it was a game, whether it was rugby or tiddlywinks, then they would go into it wanting to rub our faces in the ground and win. And how would we pick ourselves up after our near-50 point drubbing from the All Blacks?

As it happened, I was not going to be part of the action. Clive took me aside and said that the management had decided not to pick me for the play-off. He emphasised that it was definitely not a case of me being dropped but that I should remember that I was still a teenager, a teenager who had played two hard games against England and New Zealand in the space of six days. I had come out of them holding my head high. He also said that Steve (Wally) Blackmore had been with the squad since the outset and had only played the one pool game against Canada. I accepted everything that was said and, yes, with only three days to recover before the next game what was said made sense. But I won't pretend that I wasn't disappointed.

What made it doubly disappointing was that I wouldn't have the chance to play alongside the squad's latest recruit – Richard Webster. Webby arrived at the hotel after a 20-hour bus trip to Brisbane. He was in my room when Clive informed him that he was officially being invited to join the squad as a replacement for Richie Collins who had been injured and was returning home. Richard would be joining us on the flight to Rotorua. He followed the same path that I had trodden several days before, with Ray Williams and with Clive's words ringing in his ears that 'you have got to look the part'. I felt great for him, not only because he was a friend, because he deserved it on playing ability alone. He had been outstanding with the club in Canberra and, like me, I felt sure he could make the step up – but I would be watching from the stand.

Wales, of course, won the game thanks to a last-ditch try by Adrian Hadley converted from the touchline by Paul Thorburn, and now we could say that we were the third-best team in the world. This was probably the worst thing that could have happened. It was great to see Wales beat Australia in a full-scale international on New Zealand soil but at the end of the day it was nothing more than a one-off game. Technically, we had finished third in the World Cup, there was nothing wrong with being proud of that. There was a subtle difference between that, however, and kidding ourselves that we were up there with the top boys. But that's what we did and we were deceiving ourselves on a grand scale. The All Blacks had shown us (and given the opportunity France would have as well) that in terms of skills, fitness and mobility we were way behind; on another day in another situation the Wallabies would have shown us as well.

The important game, the one that more than any other we should have sat up and taken notice of, was the one against New Zealand. Two days later they beat France easily in the first World Cup final. Invited, we went to Eden Park for the match but did not venture into the stand, watching it from a bar sipping a few beers.

On the day after the final the Wales squad headed for home to be fêted as third in the world. There was no ticker-tape welcome awaiting Webby and me. We still had a contract to fulfil and returned to our flat in Canberra. That was hard and we tried everything to get out of it. We weren't seeking glory, we just wanted to go home to our families and friends.

After a roller-coaster couple of weeks during which we had dipped our toes into test rugby and hadn't disgraced ourselves we were mentally washed-out. All the extra effort made by the people at the club, although appreciated, did not make it any easier and the remaining month in Canberra dragged on as we went back to club training and playing. We did, however, see it through. At the end we were undeniably better for our summer in Australia. Then we returned home and April and I went away for two weeks in Tenerife. Halfway through the holiday I bought a British newspaper only to read that Webby had badly damaged his knee ligaments in a pre-season match. I felt sick. The summer was definitely over.

4

LEARNING HARSH LESSONS

On the face of it I had everything to look forward to at the start of the next season in Wales. I had returned from Australia as an international, Swansea were hoping to build on their success in reaching the Cup final the previous May, and Wales, as 'third in the world', were set to go from strength to strength. Despite what I've said about the foolishness of seeing ourselves as world-beaters, there was to be success, for a while at least, with the national team and I did go a long way towards proving I was worth my place in the side. That was important to me. Though nothing had been said to my face I was aware that some people would probably be saying that I had won my cap through the back door, that I was the bloke who just happened to be in the right place at the right time. If that was the case then in a way such a reaction was understandable. I knew that I could now expect to be monitored more closely but that didn't really worry me. I was feeling positive about the whole situation because I felt I had not disgraced myself in the two World Cup games. In fact what had happened in Australia had only served to send my ambitions soaring. Yet what was developing into an unsatisfactory situation at Swansea was already bringing me firmly down to earth.

What was to derail my ongoing commitment to Swansea was the club's failure to deliver one of the promises they had made to me: to find me a good job that I could build on myself to establish a secure future outside the game. During my first season it had been put on hold. I had stayed with Magnet & Southerns and, although it wasn't ideal, at least I had a regular wage and I could concentrate on my rugby. That had all changed when I agreed to go to Australia. I had resigned from the company. It had not been an easy decision to make as they had been good to me but there was never any question of them keeping a place open for me whilst I was away for the best part of four months in Canberra. From the outset Mike

James and Roger Blyth, on behalf of the Swansea committee, had told me not to worry, that there would not be a problem. When I came back from Australia there would be a new job waiting for me.

It never happened. When I met them again at pre-season training, without Richard, who was still struggling to overcome the serious knee injury he had suffered, they were full of assurances that something was in the pipeline. I could sense that nothing really was in place. I often thought of Richard, and how he would cope should he not be able to play again. April and I had visited him on our return from holiday and although we found him in pretty good spirits he was obviously worried. It was only when he went out of the room that we got the true story from his parents. He was unable to work and, not receiving any money from either employer or club, he was relying on Bill and June for all his financial needs. He had not heard from Swansea and I remember Bill saying that they had not even phoned to ask if he needed a lift to watch a game, since he was unable to drive at the time. It hit home how quickly you can go from being an international and golden boy to the forgotten man. I was more determined than ever to secure a career independent of rugby.

The situation became a huge frustration for both April and me. Luckily I did find a job as a weight training instructor at Aberdare Sports Centre. The advantage of this job was that I was able to utilise all the facilities the centre could offer to reinforce my now strict fitness regime; the disadvantage, unfortunately, was that it hardly met my criteria of long-term career prospects. As the season unfolded very little happened on the job front but my mind was taken off it to some extent by my success with Wales. This was to be a significant factor in how matters came to a head with Swansea because inevitably playing for Wales brought me into contact with people from other clubs.

One such person was Robert Norster who was playing outstandingly well in the Five Nations matches. Bob already knew that I was unhappy with Swansea. I had first got to know Bob during the World Cup, and he was captain of Cardiff. During a chat over a few drinks he suggested that a move to Cardiff would be more productive, possibly with a job thrown in. Little was happening on the Swansea front and I soon realised I would have to give this serious consideration.

Nothing summed up my annoyance with the club better than the farcical situation I was put in with a promised opening at B&Q. This was the straw that broke the camel's back. I was told that they were looking for a trainee manager and Mike arranged an interview for me. When I got there, the people at B&Q said there must have been a misunderstanding – what they were looking for was someone to stack the pallets at the back of the warehouse. I felt as if the club was were mucking me around and not taking me seriously. I rang Mike James to tell him so. I left him in no doubt that I was deeply upset.

Cardiff were not the only club that had shown interest once my unhappiness at Swansea had become apparent. I had chatted to Phil Davies who had later arranged a meeting with Norman Gale, chairman of Llanelli, on my behalf. The purpose of that meeting was to discuss a possible transfer to Llanelli and he would, through connections at the club, also help to try and secure a career in the police force. I felt that we had yet again returned to promises and, as I have already said, deep down I knew that I could never become a Scarlet so I felt that this was never really an option.

The time had come to make Swansea realise that if they couldn't help me find a job then others might. In fact Cardiff had phoned to say that there was a possible vacancy as a representative with a brewery and, more promising, there was a strong likelihood of something being arranged for me with a leasing company. News of these approaches had a remarkable effect down at St Helen's. Swansea suddenly became very active and they very quickly came up with an offer to work for Readimix Concrete. But this was a case of too little, too late; too much had happened – or not happened, in terms of taking my priorities seriously – and, to be frank, I was left with a bitter taste in my mouth.

An indication of just how things had changed was when Roger Blyth came up to Aberdare to see me at the Sports Centre, on behalf of the committee. He was obviously worried that I was thinking of leaving.

'What's the problem?' he asked, which didn't help matters because I thought it was crystal clear that the question of finding me a job had been on the agenda since day one. Roger arranged to meet me at the club for what he described as 'a 20-minute chat'. If I still wanted to go I could go with their blessing. Some chat! April took me down to St Helen's and I was expecting to have an informal discussion with one or two of the club's officials. When I entered the room there were four of them. Roger Blyth and Mike James, which was not a surprise, Dickie Moriarty, which was not a problem, and Anthony Evans, QC, which certainly was a surprise and, as things turned out, not a particularly good idea.

I should have heard the alarm bells ringing when I was introduced to

Mr Evans. He didn't waste any time in getting to the point as he saw it. With a WRU handbook in front of him he told me that if I transferred to Cardiff in order to take up an offer of employment I would be in theory making myself a professional. In the days of amateur rugby this was not acceptable. They conveniently had already forgotten that they had also promised me employment at the very beginning of my Swansea career and that was the main reason for this meeting. The other main point they made was that the club had put a lot of time into my development and that I wouldn't have won my international cap without them. I was, however, already Welsh Youth captain when I arrived at Swansea, a significant factor in their reason for signing me in the first place. I was annoyed because I had told Roger privately that I was attracted to Cardiff because of the offer of employment. I felt he had broken a confidence. I had not publicly aired my reasons for leaving and I had been under the impression that we could sort the problem out in private.

I was absolutely stunned. I had travelled down to Swansea to meet with people I regarded highly and trusted. I had taken no witness, I didn't feel I would need any, to hear the following discussions. I had attended the meeting on my own. I was informed that if I continued to push with any intended move to Cardiff, the club would make it public that I had accepted an offer of employment as an inducement. They would ensure that I would never be able to play rugby union for anyone again. This upset me greatly not only because of what they were implying but also because they had felt it necessary to approach what was meant to be a constructive meeting in such a way.

I had entered the meeting with an open mind and had certainly not made any final decision about requesting a move. Several hours later I knew that too much water had flowed under the bridge. Between one thing and another the meeting was counter-productive. It was fortunate that Dickie Moriarty was present as he was a calming influence but at the end of it I knew that my days at Swansea were numbered. April drove us home; not a word was spoken!

For a long while I was unable to justify what Swansea threatened to do to a 20-year-old who only wanted to play rugby and secure his long-term future. I could not understand it. I would like to think that they desperately wanted me to carry on playing for them and were prepared to do anything to achieve this, which in a way was a compliment to me.

It was time to talk to Cardiff again. I knew by this time that there was a job waiting for me with Jordan's Lease & Contract Hire Ltd in Barry and so as far as I was concerned it was all systems go, although Swansea had made it clear they would not grant me a transfer. I played five games on permit only for the 6th, which would mean an automatic transfer, to be refused by Swansea. It looked like I could be left in no man's land. Luckily common sense prevailed and two great Cardiff stalwarts, C.D. Williams and Alun Priday, liaised with Swansea and the Welsh Rugby Union until my transfer was completed.

I am glad to say that once everything was done and dusted normal relations were re-established. Swansea were only doing what they thought was best for Swansea Rugby Club, and that is understandable. On the other hand my first game for Cardiff against the All Whites was no picnic. There was plenty of needle and at an early ruck I was well and truly stamped on and there was no shortage of verbals, which is exactly what I had expected.

To complete the employment side of this little tale, my work with Jordan's was certainly different. By one of life's great ironies, who should also start working for them at about the same time as me but none other than Anthony Clement of Swansea. We laugh about it now but after all that happened it is worth speculating on how my club career could have continued down a different path if Swansea and not Cardiff had helped me to work for the company. I was under no illusions about it being the type of employment or company that I had been searching for during the previous two or three years. It was run by Bob Jordan and based in a garage in Barry. Clem and I got on with Bob fine and it was obvious that we were there because of his contacts with C.D. Williams, and one or two of the other committee-men at Cardiff, and Ray Williams at the Welsh Rugby Union. It was through these rugby connections that I managed to sell one or two cars but it was never going to be a big job. In fact after about a year Clem went to work at Day's in Swansea and I was left as the driver for people going to dinners and social evenings. I soon realised that it was becoming a dead-end situation and, sure enough, Jordan's hit financial trouble and I was made redundant. Once again I was out of work.

Whilst all this had been happening away from the rugby field, it was a much happier story on it. As I said it was important to me that I showed everyone that I had not won my caps on the cheap and that I could retain my place in the Wales team on merit. There was an autumn international against the USA at Cardiff Arms Park and it was reassuring that I was selected for that as a warm-up to the serious business after Christmas. The Eagles were not a great side and we won the game easily enough but it was a memorable one for me because at last the family was able to watch me playing for Wales in the flesh rather than on television from the other side of the world. To complete a happy day I scored a try on my home debut for Wales.

Although there were still a couple of months before the Five Nations fixtures got under way the encouraging fact was that there was a real feeling of continuity in the team after the World Cup campaign of the previous summer. We were a group of players that got on with one another, with young backs, a solid full-back in Paul Thorburn, several friends of mine from Swansea and my Youth days like Paul Moriarty, Robert Jones and Clem, and a core of forwards centred around Robert Norster. Most important of all was the influence of the management team of Tony Gray and Derek Quinnell. They had done a great job in the World Cup and were destined to deliver some silverware later in the season though there was not to be a happy ending to their story. They would do anything for the players and in return the players responded with an exciting brand of rugby that we all enjoyed playing.

We arrived at Twickenham in February as underdogs – again! – with Clem playing his first-ever big game at full-back and Jonathan Davies at fly-half. Paul Rendall was again my opposite number but, if anything, we won the game even more comfortably than we had the World Cup quarter-final. Jonathan Davies – or 'Jiffy' – had a marvellous match and England made the mistake of using what little ball they had to bombard Clem with high kicks. It was from one of these that he went on a daring run that was taken on by Jiffy and the backs for our left-wing Adrian Hadley to score the first of his two tries. Adolf and I became big friends as the years went by. We were at Cardiff together and then at Salford in rugby league. He was a unique player because as a wing he only ever did just enough to score the tries. He never believed in expending unnecessary energy – which is probably why he never beat me by more than a yard in sprint training. And Adolf is a great guy to have around when the anoraks and hangers-on move in when we're trying to relax. At first he is unfailingly polite but if they outstay their welcome Adolf's inevitable response is a surprised look and the trademark put-down, 'You're still here, are you?' It never fails.

With England disposed of we returned to the Arms Park for our game with Scotland. It turned out to be another cracker, remembered for a try by Jiffy and another by Ieuan Evans when he side-stepped several times off his left foot to score at the posts. It was a brilliant effort and of all the wings I played with only he could have scored it. I think I am right in saying it was Ieuan's first international season. I remember thinking that he looked quite slow at the first of many training sessions, (slow you understand compared to a prop). I later found out that Ieuan didn't waste all his energy on the training pitch, unless it was absolutely necessary, but saved it for the real game where there were not many who could live with him.

It was a game I particularly enjoyed because it was my first experience of propping against David Sole. Though we obviously didn't know it at the time, a year later he and I were to form two-thirds of a Lions' Test front row. I have to say that after that first 80 minutes against him I was very impressed. Somewhere along the line David seemed to have picked up a reputation of being good in the loose but not much of a tight-forward. I can put everybody right on that misconception. He could certainly scrummage with the best of them, and he did so at every scrum, which is not always the case. There was one simple reason why he was also so mobile – it was because he was incredibly fit. One thing in my favour in that game was that our hooker, Kevin Phillips, had not finished the Twickenham match and his replacement Ian Watkins had kept his place in our side. There is no disrespect towards Kevin in this – in many ways he was the better all-round player – but Ian was one of the best technical hookers I ever encountered. He hooked really low in the scrum and that took a lot of the pressure off me. He was also pretty lively in the loose and featured prominently in a stirring final 20 minutes when we came back to win the game, finishing off with a couple of drop goals by Jiffy.

Now the Triple Crown was in sight and we went to Dublin quietly confident. The Irish, as always, were fired up and there was no shortage of knees and elbows flying around off the ball. They had clearly targeted Robert Norster as our main source of lineout ball and his opposite number Willie Anderson was not slow in coming forward to answer the call to arms. I couldn't blame them for doing it because Bob was having an outstanding season. He had completely dominated Wade Dooley at Twickenham and had eventually sorted out the Scots after a shaky start at Cardiff. He was clobbered at the first lineout in Dublin and the game turned into a bit of a dogfight. In the end we sneaked it with a late penalty by Paul Thorburn. We had won the first Triple Crown for Wales in nine years and we soon learnt what was meant by the weight of expectation as the build-up began immediately for what everyone was already calling the Grand Slam match against France a fortnight later.

What happened during those two weeks was probably second nature to the great sides of ten years before but this was a new experience for all of us. We were a young team and, looking back, the match and the anticipation surrounding it probably came a year too soon in our development. We lost by a single point against a not particularly good French side. All season we had played an open style of rugby but the weather was dreadful and we were also heavily penalised. My own rugby education continued as I was up against Louis Armary. He was not particularly big but he had his own methods for winning games. The right side of my rib cage was black after the match because he had pinched me all the way through it. I think I was supposed to have reacted and thrown a few punches but that would have been fatal. Instead I blew kisses to Monsieur Armary.

Wales and France finished joint top of the Five Nations table but the international season was by no means over. We were now due to go on an eight-match tour of New Zealand, a challenge that seemed exciting enough at the time but, with hindsight, we needed like a hole in the head. We were certainly not afraid of the challenge and to take on the All Blacks would be a good test of our progress. The mood in Wales was distinctly upbeat. After all, we were third in the world – that was still being quoted – and we had won the Triple Crown. This was a bad case of selective memory because we had also lost by nearly 50 points to New Zealand and the word was that, a year on, their current crop was even better.

The tour turned out to be a disaster. Perhaps we were never expected to win the two tests but neither was it thought that 'nearly 50 points' in 1987 would become 'over 50 points' – twice – in 1988. The greater disaster was the effect it had on the confidence of our players and the repercussions for the coaching staff. There is no point now in making excuses. We were not the first touring team in New Zealand to find ourselves in poor hotels – in our case on one occasion in the middle of an industrial estate – or to experience poor training facilities. What was hard to take was the realisation that we were out of our depth. The World Cup champions of a year before had stepped up to an even higher level and we had fallen even further behind.

Our cause was not helped by a succession of injuries and there was the distinct impression that one or two of our walking wounded showed signs of relief at being flown home early. I myself had received a nasty but unintentional knee to my forehead during a game against Taranaki and cannot remember anything about leaving the field, helped along by the physio. Apparently the boys on the bench were in hysterics because he was trying to take me off along the half-way line and I wanted to go the other way. I also had several stitches sewn into one of my ears to hold it on. To this day I have to be careful because there is very little skin remaining to play with behind my left ear should it come off again.

And there were one or two other features of being in New Zealand that really got under our skin. The first, undoubtedly, was the attitude of the All Blacks towards us. They were very arrogant and they certainly didn't mix with us. Fair enough, they put 50 points on the board against us twice in as many weeks but that was no excuse for Gary Whetton refusing to exchange his jersey at the end of a test match. Their attitude was best summed up by his brother, Alan, at the post-match dinner when he left his table and picked up the microphone and asked in full voice, 'Can we get on with this? We want to go out and enjoy ourselves.'

At the second Test in Auckland a trumpeter played 'The Last Post', which says as much about their sense of humour as their manners and when we were out and about in our Wales blazers we were actually laughed at. Like the Australians, the Kiwis thrive on success and there is nothing wrong with that. They love their rugby and you can't help but be impressed when you go to their schools and see the enthusiasm, the organisation and the advanced skills that are everywhere throughout the age groups. In 1988 they were way ahead of everyone but it wouldn't be stretching the point to say that although they were undoubtedly the best team in the world, they still had a lot to learn about dignity and respect for their opponents.

There were a few exceptions. In the tests I renewed acquaintances with Steve McDowell and Sean Fitzpatrick. It was just like old times I packed low and they threw punches! I think there was a grudging respect because afterwards Steve invited me into their changing-room for a drink. He was physically immense and very quick and nothing had changed my opinion from our first encounter in the World Cup that he was the best loose-head I had ever come up against.

Long before the tour finished we accepted that we had lessons to learn from the New Zealanders. Sadly the energies of the powers-that-be were spent on dishing out blame rather than devising plans for the future. To the dismay of all the players the axe fell on Tony Gray and Derek Quinnell. This was typical of how we as a nation change direction at the drop of a hat. One minute we are beating our chests and proclaiming that we are number three in the world and Triple Crown winners. Then next, the men who guided us to those successes are ditched. Both Tony and Derek acknowledged that New Zealand held the top-dog spot. They also knew that we could learn from them. They even went to an All Blacks' training session during the tour and they wanted to put what they had seen into their plans for the future. They never got the chance. We were sad to see them go and as things turned out the results for the national team in the years that followed were worse not better.

The end of the New Zealand tour coincided with the end of my time at Swansea. I arrived back in Wales ready to start my new club career at Cardiff and also very aware that there were a lot of pieces to pick up with Wales. There was a Lions' tour looming on the horizon at the end of the new domestic season and if all went well there was just a chance that ten months later I might be flying south again on what might turn out to be a far more successful trip.

5

A LION CUB

To become a British Lion will always be the ultimate ambition of every player in the home countries and I was no different, but the longer the 1988–89 season went on the more unlikely my prospects seemed. To begin with the Wales team hit a really rough patch. In the autumn internationals we struggled to beat Western Samoa in the days before they had become a force to be reckoned with and then, a month later, came the real calamity when we lost at home to Romania. Now the knives were out with a vengeance and the side effects were catastrophic. Jonathan Davies had captained the side and he bore the brunt of the criticism. He decided that enough was enough and shortly after Christmas he went north to play rugby league with Widnes. A big blow for Wales and I suspect that, deep down, Jiffy would have hoped to stay in union for at least another season so he could become a Lion.

My own chances took a dive early in the New Year. Wales lost again at Murrayfield and I failed to finish the game after partially tearing a ligament in my left knee. WRU surgeon Malcolm Downes put it in plaster and I was told I would be on crutches for six weeks. Suddenly the Lions' tour was only around the corner and I seemed destined to miss it. There was no possibility of me playing in the remaining home internationals and everything became a race against time. With the Five Nations continuing whilst I was sidelined it was very much a case of being out of the limelight and out of mind. It was very frustrating. My spirits were lifted slightly when I received a letter checking my availability for the tour. Then as the time to announce the squad drew ever nearer the newspapers were full of predictions about the likely selections. With Wales losing to both Ireland and France it was hardly surprising that very few Welshmen figured in the guesswork. That changed slightly when England were beaten in Cardiff but I was still not involved. One encouraging sign was that at least one journalist, Stephen Jones in *The Sunday Times*, wrote that I should be picked for my scrummaging and mobility. For my own part I still felt I was a strong candidate.

The day finally arrived when the official announcement was due to be made. There are many ways of finding out whether you are selected. In 1997 I received a letter. I have seen it on television as happened in 2001, but in 1989 I sat in a car park in Barry frantically trying to find a sports bulletin on the radio. In fact Bob Jordan was with me and it was more his idea than mine. I was very apprehensive because if my name was not on the list then it would be fairly embarrassing. What would the two of us do – climb out of the car and go back to work?

We were still sitting there twiddling with the wavelengths when Bob's secretary, Karen, came out of the office to say that Ray Williams, secretary to the WRU, had phoned to congratulate me on becoming a Lion. Ray has always been one of the first to congratulate me on every success. When I was appointed captain of Wales I received a letter of congratulations. The relief was indescribable. I was still only 21 and in some ways the enormity of becoming a Lion so quickly (after all it was only two years before that I had gone to Canberra with Richard Webster to play club rugby and do odd jobs) hadn't fully sunk in. I immediately phoned my parents and April and the celebrations began.

Before I went home to Aberdare, however, Bob Jordan insisted on a more immediate congratulatory drink in Cardiff. It was all very civilised. He took me to Le Monde, a popular French restaurant in the city, but when we got there another Lion had beaten us to it. Bob Norster was already there with one of his business associates, Aly Thomas. It was great news that Bob was also on the tour because as well as being my club captain he had been a Lion six years before, and in my year at Cardiff he and his wife Kath had become great friends of April and me. Bob is a good man to have in any team. Not only does he bring his vast experience, he also brings a great sense of support – as I was to discover again in the months ahead.

He was always there with words of encouragement and was a perfectionist himself in everything he did. More than anything Bob wants success and with his immaculate dress sense and dry wit he was a superb tourist. We stayed in the restaurant and were wined and dined for several hours and then moved across to the clubhouse at the Arms Park. Day became night, as someone once said, and my last memory of a big day in my rugby life was being put in a taxi by Aly Thomas with his clear instruction to the driver to take this valuable Lion home to Aberdare.

Now the hard work began. I was on the tour but I still had to prove my fitness. A particular priority was to improve my stamina so most lunchtimes I went to see the club's fitness coach, Gwynne Griffiths. There would be bleep and sprint tests facing me before I could be sure I would be on the plane to Australia. I also needed to play some club rugby. I had already played three times for Cardiff during March but my plans in that direction were blown out of the water when we went to Bristol in the same week as the Lions' squad was announced. I received a blow on my hand when making a tackle and immediately realised that it was a major knock. In fact I had broken my right thumb. The club's doctor, Roger Evans, said it would need to be in plaster for six weeks to which I replied, 'No chance!' I wasn't going to miss the tour for anything and, playing down the seriousness of the fracture, the cast came off inside a month and Roger applied strapping instead. The seriousness of the break was kept out of the papers for obvious reasons. By the end of May I was fit enough to head for Weybridge and the squad's final pre-tour preparation.

There were going to be seven Welsh players on the tour – Ieuan Evans, Mike Hall, John Devereux, Robert Jones, Mike Griffiths, Bob Norster and myself – plus Clive Rowlands as manager. Clive had started his organising activities early and had hired a bus to take us up the M4. I was picked up at the Whitchurch roundabout in Cardiff with Mike Griffiths. As with Bob, it was great to have Griff with us. He was another family friend who the following year would ask April and me to act as godparents to Luc, his youngest son. The farewells were particularly painful for his wife, Ann, who was expecting Luc at the time. She, together with Joel their first son and April, waved us off as we boarded the bus. We headed for the excitement and anticipation of the Lions' get-together as the two women and Joel retired to the nearest Asda café with one of them, at least, shedding tears by the bucketful.

We spent a week at Weybridge and amidst all the hustle and bustle of making sure everything was in place for our departure, and also the anxiety of any late injury scares, there was the important matter of getting to know each other. From the very first day the signs of togetherness were obvious. Having more or less shaken off my own worries I could understand the struggles that Gareth Chilcott was having with his own leg injury. We all got behind him and there was relief all round when Gareth reached the required standard on the bleep test to be passed fit for the tour two days before lift off. Unlike two or three of the previous Lions' tours no one was being sent home at the eleventh hour.

In the weeks since my selection I had had enough time to consider my own approach to the challenge ahead. I came to the conclusion that I was there on merit but also realised that I had achieved the ultimate honour very early in my career – I was the youngest-ever Lions' prop – whereas other players had slogged for ten years or more to be where I was. Ambition and determination had driven me ever since my early days and I had reached a stage where I already had a couple of seasons of international rugby behind me and I was a strong scrummager as well as mobile. So I was upbeat about what lay ahead.

I also felt a real tingle of excitement that I would be training and playing with so many people I looked up to. First and foremost there was the possibility of being in the same test front row as David Sole who had made such a big impression on me in the Scottish internationals I had played in. We had also briefly played together for the Barbarians against the Wallabies the previous November and we had packed so low that their hooker Tommy Lawton was forced to take down four scrums. Now there was the prospect of forming a unit with him for an extended period. That excited me and when the tour got under way he did not disappoint me. He was phenomenal, and it didn't take me long to realise that there were many benefits from teaming up with him in training. A front row fraternity soon emerged. Mike Griffiths and I went back years and Coochie turned out to be a revelation. He was my main contender for a test place at tight-head but he was very helpful to me at all times. Once the die was cast and I won that test place he threw himself heart and soul into watching me play and then offering advice. That summed up all that was good about the 1989 Lions – and, of course, with Coochie in particular there was that unique West Country humour which he was famed for. His effect on team morale was incalculable.

I also became a big admirer of Brian Moore. Here was Old Pitbull himself, in the flesh – the archetypal Englishman. Except that he wasn't. Brian was an amazing character. He was fiercely competitive on the field, totally committed to winning, and a magnificent hooker whose low positioning helped me a great deal as my technique is very similar. Brian always completed extra personal training after organised training sessions. Off the field he was someone who could talk with people from all walks of life and be superb company. I didn't know him at all before the tour but by the end of it I was proud to say that I had been part of the best front-row combination I could ever hope to play with. It really motivated me, seeing David and Brian at their best and being there with them in the big matches.

Deep inside me there was another great incentive. Before we had even left London there were stories appearing in the press to the effect that I was lucky to be in the squad. The former England and Lions' captain Bill Beaumont was quoted as saying that I was a possible weak link and the Aussie coach Bob Dwyer took the criticism a bit further and was of the opinion that my scrummaging technique was illegal. Here we go again, I thought. I had got under the skin of Steve McDowell and the All Blacks' front row in the previous two summers and with David Sole and the Lions' other hooker, Steve Smith from Ireland, we had dominated the Wallabies for the Barbarians. Dwyer was obviously intent on getting his retaliation in early. If there was any hint of a problem in the scrum his comments would be at the back of the referees' minds and we could be whistled out of a test match. As for Beaumont, he was entitled to his opinion but, as a guy who had led the Lions himself only nine years before in South Africa, he should have been aware that on any tour some players prove unexpectedly successful. Being British and not English he might have given me the benefit of the doubt but he didn't, so it was up to me to prove him – and Dwyer – wrong.

When we reached Australia our manager, Clive Rowlands, had the foresight to invite one of their leading officials, Bob Fordham, to talk to us about the likely Australian interpretation of a new scrummaging law. This was the one which insisted on four stages to joining a scrum: crouch, touch, pause and engage. With safety in mind the intention was to stop front rows charging into each other. It had been introduced by the law makers the previous year but had not been rigidly enforced in the northern hemisphere. Fordham was a former international referee himself and his meeting with us was useful. The only grey area, according to him, was the 'pause' element but our forwards' coach, Roger Uttley, felt sure that there would be no problems once the tour was under way.

It didn't take long for me to be thrown in, what looked on paper at least, the deep end. Our first game was in Perth against Western Australia. They were by no means the strongest side we were due to meet but, if you believed the hype, I was about to be taken to the cleaners by their loose-head, a 20-stone-plus former All Black by the name of Paul Koteka. As it happened the team selected for the tour-opener included what turned out to be our test front row three weeks later but I would like to think that whoever was playing alongside me I could have sorted out Koteka. The feeling in the changing-room before the game was unique in my experience. Only Bob Norster and Donal Lenihan in the second row had been Lions before, and that was six long years before on a difficult campaign in New Zealand. We were opening a new chapter in Lions' history with the first full tour of Australia in nearly a century. Putting on the red jersey for the first time in that quiet changing-room every single one of us, even Bob and Donal, were totally motivated. We suspected that the local side would throw the kitchen sink at us but they were not a class outfit and our pre-tour instructions had been to show complete self-discipline and that's exactly what we did. They niggled us or, at least, they *tried* to niggle us but we played the rugby and won the game 44–0.

The sweetest moment came when we shoved the home pack back over their line for a pushover try. We also took three tight-heads in the game and the only answer from Koteka and his front row was to take the scrum down. I felt I had produced a big performance myself and, though it was by no means what was foremost in my mind, I couldn't help but think I had taken the first steps towards justifying my place in the squad. That didn't stop Bob Dwyer and his friends in the Aussie press from having a go at me. Even the Western Australian coach Viv Booker joined in, saying that the Lions would be well advised to move Mike Griffiths across to the tight-head to improve the scrummaging. As for Dwyer the needle was stuck – my technique was illegal and I was collapsing scrums. There was only one way for me to react to this sort of barrage and that was to get on with my game and prove myself again and again in the matches ahead. I left Perth with a smile on my face when one of the journalists covering the tour was astute enough to write that Koteka's 'considerable stomach' usually hit the floor before his head!

I was chuckling even more a couple of weeks later after we had beaten Queensland. Who should I bump into but Mr Bob Dwyer. It was one of those moments when two individuals can't avoid speaking to one another but I was only too happy to look him in the eye. He returned the eye contact and said, 'Well done.'

The way the management had approached that first game was typical of what happened throughout the trip. I've mentioned the manager, Clive Rowlands. At first glance he appeared the most unsuitable appointment imaginable. The Lions are all about putting aside Welsh, Scottish, Irish and English identities and becoming *British* Lions. And here was Clive, the most passionate of Welshmen, who two years before in Australia had said in the wake of our World Cup stuffing by the All Blacks that we would simply go back home and beat England every season, taking charge of a multi-national team. What could they have been thinking of? Well, I can say it from the head as well as the heart that Clive Rowlands was absolutely ideal. That passion for Wales became a passion for the Lions. He is totally steeped in rugby history and tradition and the old values and from the outset we were 'his boys'. He was absolutely marvellous. He loved to talk and, God, could he talk! Everything centred on the pride in being a Lion. 'Be proud of this badge!' became his catch phrase and we loved him because he was 100 per cent behind the players.

If the pre-tour perceptions were that Clive Rowlands would be all things Welsh then the worries about our assistant coach Roger Uttley were that he would be pro-English. Whoever thought that should have known better. Here was one of the great England forwards of his generation who had been a test player in what was generally regarded as the best Lions' team ever, the one that went to South Africa in 1974 and returned home unbeaten in 22 matches. He was also one of the most level-headed blokes you could ever wish to meet. He had a background in teaching but, unlike some of his profession, he was a listener as well as a talker. With very few exceptions we all took to him very early on. He obviously knew his stuff as a forwards' coach and had achieved some limited success in the England set-up. With the Lions, and what we liked to think was the cream of the forward talent available, he flourished. The only blot was that a couple of Welsh forwards retained dark suspicions about him. Mike Griffiths, unfortunately, didn't get on with him. I found this particularly hard because during this tour Griff and I had become increasingly close, training and socialising together so much that the others took great delight in teasing us about it. Griff felt he didn't get the chances or the credit he deserved. David Sole, Brian Moore and I were the favoured unit in the build-up to the first Test in the front row while we all felt that Roger was pushing Wade Dooley at Bob Norster's expense. Griff did pack down with Brian and me against New South Wales but after that he was always in the mid-week team. Sadly I think it was a case of a clash of personalities between Roger and Griff. Years later on my second Lions' tour I was to experience a similar thing with Jim Telfer of Scotland.

The star of the show was undoubtedly Ian McGeechan. In the years since 1989 he has come to be regarded, quite rightly, as the greatest Lions' coach ever but it is easy to forget the challenge facing him on our tour. All eyes were on him as everyone wondered if he was up to the task. He was helped by the quality of the people around him but the success he achieved then and in later years was firmly down to his own ability. Geech was incredibly well-organised and everything he put in place went like clockwork. He was wonderful with us as individuals as he met us one by one and would chat about anything. The bottom line of his success as a coach however revolved around what went on at the training field. He introduced more ball skills sessions than I had ever encountered and in our six weeks in Australia every session was varied and specifically aimed at the next game.

Once we had disposed of Western Australia in the first game we flew across to the east coast and the real business of the tour began. We had some tough matches against Queensland and New South Wales, as we had expected, but reached Sydney for the first Test unbeaten. Having seen all the players that Australia would be likely to call on in the provincial matches we were confident, but not over-confident, that we could win the three-match test series. The local press wrote with hostility about our style of play and there was a lot of talk about us being a dirty team.

We had dominated the Queensland front row up at Brisbane, and they were the chosen front row pencilled in for the Australian test team. Much the same happened against New South Wales. Perhaps we were kidding ourselves but we had the feeling that the Australians were panicking a bit about who to put in their front row.

The only scare I had was not about what might happen on the field but what had actually happened in a river in Cairns. It nearly brought my tour – and a lot more – to a premature end. No rugby tour is ever complete without afternoons and occasional days off from training and playing when you can see a bit of the country you're visiting and also enjoy some recreation. That very nearly went wrong for me when several of us went white-water rafting in the Baron Gorge. Now I have to admit that this was something new to me. You don't get many chances to go over the rapids in the Cynon Valley. The normal spare-time options on tour usually involve golf or fishing or karting but this seemed too good a day out to turn down. The only down side seemed to be a one-and-a-half hour journey to reach the river but there was worse than that to come. Roger Uttley, Mike Teague, Derek White, Rory Underwood, Bob

Norster and I climbed into an inflatable raft with the local instructor and we immediately realised that this was not going to be a calm cruise upstream. There was a heck of a swell in the water, in fact it was one grade away from being too dangerous to ride.

There was a lot of laughter at first even though there was nothing in the raft to hold on to, as the water became even rougher. Then we reached the white water. The instructor's advice had seemed sound enough. If we came out of the raft we were to stay on the left of the river, away from the rocks on the right, and let the current carry us to the bank. Sure enough, out we came, but as the four others swam to safety on the left, Mike Teague and I were swept helplessly to the right. Before I could do anything I realised I was being pushed by the force of the water against a concave rock and, to all intents and purposes, I was trapped, going under and coming up again with no way of escaping. Mike was holding onto a rock and trying to reach out to me but I was taking in water and there was a real danger of blacking-out.

The laughing on the bank had stopped and the instructor was running around, shouting instructions and throwing a rope into the water. I remember him screaming, 'Don't let the water take you under the rock!' but I was helpless to stop it doing just that. This must have carried on for at least five minutes and I was swallowing water all the time. It had happened so quickly, there was no sense of fear. Afterwards I pondered what might have happened if finally the current hadn't changed in my favour and I had gone so limp that the force of the river flipped me out. It seems that if I had kept fighting I could easily have been pushed under the rock and drowned. Thankfully, Mike was able to grab my arm and help me to safety but I was really shaken. Later we were told that a Japanese tourist had drowned in similar circumstances at the same rock a month before. Wonderful! I can still see Bob Norster's face on the bank as I was flailing around – one minute he was as red as a beetroot with laughter, the next he was as white as a sheet. After that anything, including the Aussie pack, would be a doddle.

So, still alive and kicking, we knuckled down to our preparations for the test match. The criticism of our style of play reached new heights in the local press but that didn't concern us. I was delighted to win selection alongside Brian Moore and David Sole and we were surprised that the Queensland props, Crowley and Lillicrap would be against us with Tommy Lawton at hooker. We had no worries about them but what unhinged us on the day was our lineout. Some wrong calls were made when we were in attacking positions. With the benefit of hindsight it wasn't very clever to throw long balls in such positions – and as a result Bob Norster won only two balls in the entire match. That was to have a devastating effect on the rest of his tour with Roger still pursuing Wade Dooley's selection. In the end we went down almost without a whimper with Australia scoring early on and never looking back to win 30–12. We were badly shaken.

The week between the first two tests produced more pressure than I had ever experienced in my life. We were written off as no-hopers in the Australian press and there were one or two issues flying around with the management concerning adequate training facilities. For the players, though, it was all about nervous energy. We knew we had let ourselves down in Sydney and that had led to worries about who might lose their places in the starting line-up for the second Test in Brisbane. And anything short of a win would mean the series was lost and we would be labelled as a failure for years to come.

There was also a mid-week game in Canberra against Australian Capital Territory and I was named as a replacement. I was reasonably confident that I would keep my place in the test team but also on the bench was Bob Norster and there was already speculation that he was about to be dropped for the first time in his career. That was exactly what happened when the team was finally named on the Saturday morning – our management received a hammering for not publicly announcing the selection sooner. The mid-week team had done well to run up 40 points against ACT after trailing by 14 points at one stage and Wade Dooley had done enough to win Bob's place. I had had a run out against ACT, coming on as a replacement for Gareth Chilcott. This was seen as a really important win, a win that put the tour back on track and very important for us going into the second Test.

The thinking was that Wade was sufficiently big and heavy to take on Bill Campbell who had won the majority of lineout ball in the first Test. Bob was not amused. Although we were again criticised for what was called a mediocre display a win was a win and most of us were in good heart when we reached Brisbane.

The first half of that second Test was as rough as it gets in international rugby. There were fights breaking out all over the place and even the two scrum-halves, Robert Jones and the Wallaby skipper Nick Farr-Jones, were going at each other hammer and tongs in the first five minutes. We were cancelling out their lineout threat very effectively by taking their main jumper, Cutler, to the ground but the problem was that when he hit the deck he wasn't releasing the ball. A player doing that consistently can either be heavily penalised or expect a right shoeing. The first wasn't going to happen because although I was shouting at the French referee, René Hourquet, who couldn't speak English, Cutler was continually allowed to kill the ball.

There was no shortage of verbals – Cutler invited me to do something about him not releasing the ball. So I did. The next time he went down, I went in with my feet aiming at the ball, which he was still holding in his hands. But as the bodies piled in around him I lost sight of him and reaching with my foot my boot caught the back of Cutler's head instead of his hands. At that point pandemonium broke out. The Kiwi touch judge Keith Lawrence had come onto the pitch and as he was talking to the referee Lawton came charging at me throwing punches. Hourquet gave both Lawton and me a dressing-down and we got on with our game. Campbell, however, spent the rest of the match whingeing so I nicknamed him 'Shirley Campbell'. That went down like a lead balloon.

As for the match, we had the distinct impression that the Australians had lost their appetite for a dog fight after their first-half mauling and we scored two late tries to snatch a great victory. Then the repercussions started. Ian McGeechan and Clive Rowlands saw me the following day with the captain, Finlay Calder, also in attendance. They felt that the aggression with which we had gone into the game had gone too far, but at the same time they knew I wasn't an idiot who went looking to kick a player in the head. They then issued a statement saying that I had been reprimanded and warned about my future conduct at the same time noting that there had been retaliation by Tommy Lawton. I don't think for one minute that the Australians would consider themselves totally innocent, especially as they could be seen to have started a few of the flare-ups. It seemed to me that the hardest thing for them to swallow was that they lost most of them. This was too good an opening for Clive to miss and he added that he hoped the Australian management would speak to their players as well.

That did nothing to calm down the controversy raging around my head. All sorts of things were being said and written: I should be sent home; I should never play for Wales again; I was a stamper and I should be outlawed from the game. It went on and on. It became so bad that the Lions' management thought that it would be better if I did not train with the rest of the squad, because the training pitch was constantly surrounded by the Australian media. I found all this hard to believe as Australia had made a hero out of Steve Finnare, a prop who broke Graham Price's jaw with an unprovoked punch from behind in 1978. I had already gone on record in interviews after the test saying that I was not trying to maim Cutler, but I had refused to apologise for the way our pack had set about our task. I admitted that we were psyched up and that we knew that we could beat them by playing it hard and fair and knocking the wind out of them. Three weeks before Queensland had shown us that they did not like the direct approach and it had worked again. The Australian pack had been knocked back on the drive and their backs had played behind the gain line and I forecast there would be a repeat of this in the final test when we returned to Sydney. No one could accuse me of sitting on the fence!

Not that the Australians were shrinking violets themselves. Lawton gave it the full works in one of his own interviews. He was quoted as saying that I was a young prop of 22 who was still a 16-year-old between the ears and that all the Lions' forwards reminded him of schoolboys on holiday because away from home they thought they could get away with anything. He didn't stop at that, going on to say that one or two of us were making the game look like a zoo and that we didn't respect the uniform we were wearing. And to think that the next test was less than a week away – it obviously wasn't going to be a garden party!

The Australian Rugby Union became officially involved when they announced that they were preparing a video which they claimed showed unacceptable incidents from the test prejudicial to the best interests of rugby. They intended sending this video nasty to the Four Home Unions in London for their information and to help them with any action they thought appropriate. What was interesting about that statement was that it also said that they would recommend to the International Board that in future video evidence should be used as part of the game's judicial system. So out of the mayhem came a suggestion that over ten years later would be introduced into top-class rugby.

As things worked out, if it wasn't quite a case of everything being sweetness and light in the third Test, it was certainly less violent than had been anticipated by the doom-mongers who had forecast all-out war. Shirley Campbell, true to form, moaned his way through the entire 80 minutes of what was in fact a fine match that we sneaked by a single point. We put ourselves into a strong position of being 19–12 ahead with 20 minutes left, but it was a long 20 minutes. Wade Dooley had damaged a knee, David Sole had been stamped on by David Campese (yes, even the Australians could stoop to that sort of thing). This particular incident had gone totally unreported in the Australian press and was completely brushed under the carpet even though David himself believed he was very close to losing his eye. I was suffering from badly bruised ribs. No one, though, was going to leave the field unless he was stretchered off. A couple of quick penalties had reduced the margin to a single point but our defence in those final minutes, as the Australians ran everything, was incredible. The relief and the satisfaction at the final whistle were overwhelming. We had come back from one down to win a three-match series and we had made history.

For reasons that were not entirely clear, the tour planners had arranged for us to spend another week in Australia after the real business was over. We won a meaningless up-country match by over 70 points and then returned to Sydney one more time to play against an ANZAC XV. Apparently it was an attempt to create a fixture similar to the Barbarians-against-touring-team matches back home so I suppose the extra, unwanted week was no different from what the Wallabies and others had been subjected to for years in the UK. Our opponents were a combination of Australians and All Blacks and we won again but I only lasted 11 minutes before my damaged ribs finally sent me off. At least it gave Mike Griffiths an opportunity to play in the nearest thing to a full-blown Lions' test match.

Then at long last it was time to fly home. I was returning with the rest of the team and not, as some had wanted, a fortnight earlier, banished in isolation and disgrace. Six months later I would be setting out on a much shorter journey, from South Wales to the north of England, that in some people's eyes was the same as being banished. I was about to switch from rugby union to rugby league.

6

THE LEAGUE YEARS

The journey is barely 250 miles by road and when businessmen or holidaymakers travel from Cardiff to Yorkshire they can always turn around and make the return journey as and when they please. In 1990, however, the trip from union to league for players was strictly a one-way ticket. For that reason, if no other, it was not a journey to be taken lightly. Rugby league is a great game and many Welsh players before me had made the big break and headed north in search of fame and fortune. Most of them had gone by choice but a great number had done so because of sheer economic necessity. I was very much one of the latter camp – though it was a move that I subsequently didn't regret one little bit. It is usually the backs, like Jonathan Davies, Scott Gibbs and David Watkins, who do well when they change over to the 13-a-side code but it is much harder for forwards, especially props like myself, to successfully adjust their games.

To be absolutely honest, the prospect of a move to the north of England to start a new life, which was what it would be, in a totally alien game, was never high on my agenda. After all, what would I, who at 22 was already a British Lion and had been part of a Wales Triple Crown team, have to gain from such a move? Money, would be the quick answer, and I wouldn't deny it. To be more accurate, it was more a case of security for both April and me. In the long autumn between my return from the Lions' tour and the start of the Five Nations' matches the following January, I found myself squeezed into a corner where eventually the decision to sign on the dotted line for Leeds Rugby League Club was made for me. We had a mortgage to pay, I was unemployed and too proud to sign on at the dole, promises had been broken by the Cardiff club and the Welsh Rugby Union seemed unable to help. Frankly, I was weary of those broken promises in particular and in the end we travelled north with a sense of relief rather than disappointment.

It could all have been so different. The new season with Cardiff had started well and off the field I had found a job that at last seemed to be going some way towards establishing some sort of career. I had answered an advert in *The Western Mail* for a vacancy as a recruitment consultant with a company called Manpower in a section called Overdrive, based in Queen Street in the city. I enjoyed the work quite a bit. It involved interviewing drivers and then finding them work. The only problem was that I was responsible for paying them their wages every Wednesday and in those days more often than not Cardiff had mid-week games.

It was a case of juggling my time so that drivers received their money on the day they expected it and then I could concentrate on whatever Wednesday fixture we had. Everything worked fine when there was a home match since I was literally five minutes away from the Arms Park. Away games were not so straightforward. The crunch came when we were playing at Pontypool with a seven o'clock kick-off. I didn't travel on the team coach as I had to wait for the last drivers to come in for their pay-packets. It was a mad rush and I didn't arrive at Pontypool Park until 15 minutes before kick-off. After the game, which we won, the coach Alan Phillips took me to one side and told me that arriving that late was not good enough and it was up to the club to sort out new job arrangements.

That was fair enough and the club's commercial manager Albert Francis assured me that the club would, as he put it, 'find me something better'. In the meantime they would pay our mortgage, as they were confident that it would only be a week or two. I was reluctant to resign from Overdrive but after several tellings-off for being late and several more assurances that an alternative could be found I handed in my notice. That was a big mistake. April and I had bought a house in Aberaman and the bills were coming in thick and fast. She was working in Cardiff as a training officer for Mid-Glamorgan County Council but suddenly I was out of work again. There was no sign of the promised job or the assistance with the mortgage and in the months leading up to Christmas the club arranged only one interview for me, with a brewery. This was the Swansea scenario all over again. We had enough to cover the first four months but after that we could see real problems in meeting our financial commitments.

Purely by coincidence, an old friend of mine, Les Miles of Mountain Ash, turned up at our front door one evening to deliver some groggs that John Hughes of The Grogg Shop, Pontypridd, had made for me. Les had connections with several rugby league clubs in the north and he said that Warrington were interested in my joining them and asked me to consider it. I was in no position to do otherwise but at that stage expressed no great interest to Les. My union career was still very important to me. I had played three games against the All Blacks for Cardiff, Wales and the Barbarians in recent weeks. The first match of the Five Nations against France was around the corner but if I was to play at my best I needed to sort out my financial worries sooner rather than later.

I knew that Cardiff – and for that matter the Welsh Rugby Union – were anxious for me to stay so it seemed the ideal time to put the ball firmly back in their court. The Union had been making promises for some time about a post as a development officer under their director of coaching, John Dawes, with whom I had been working closely on a voluntary basis. I had therefore gained the relevant experience to make me the ideal candidate for the post. An appointment was due to be made in December. That did not happen and now it was being suggested, by the committee, that a *possible* decision would be made by the following May. It was another case of ifs and buts. So now the only hope of me staying in South Wales lay with the club. I had resigned from Overdrive on the firm promise of something else being found for me. Where was it? In desperation I went back to Albert Francis and asked for the financial help to tide me over. His response was again positive – there was a committee meeting on the Monday evening and everything would be sorted out.

The following week I went back to see him and as soon as I went into the room I could sense something was wrong. Albert was not his usual bubbly self; neither was Bob Norster who was there with him in his role as club captain. The committee had voted against any financial help, however short term, to help me out. Both Bob and Albert were visibly disappointed with the U-turn of the committee. Both of them assured me they were doing their best to get me job interviews but I would have to be patient. I could see their and the committee's point of view – but patience didn't pay the bills. I had not been sitting back waiting for the club to find a job for me but what I experienced was that when prospective employers became aware of the time off I would need they immediately went cold. In that economic climate it was understandable.

I felt well and truly cornered. So when Les Miles approached me a second time there was only one thing I could say, I was seriously thinking about a transfer to rugby league. A few days later he was back again with the news that not only Warrington but also Leeds were interested in me. He had spoken to the chairmen of both clubs and Leeds had said they would better any offer made by Warrington. I played for Wales against France on the Saturday and in the week that followed there was a flurry of activity. The Leeds chairman Bernard Colby flew down with their coach, David Ward, to meet with me and Les in the airport hotel outside Cardiff. There was a fifth person present – Tony Clement.

Leeds wanted Clem as well and he was very interested. For me that was great news as the move would not seem such a wrench if my old pal was there with me. Not that it would be the deciding factor. April and I had already talked everything through over and over again. Her agreement was essential to any final decision and, as always, she was magnificently supportive. Even though she had recently been promoted in her own career it was typical of her to say if it was what I wanted she would support any decision I made. She was always a person with a sense of adventure!

There was still a lot of talking to do. I have to admit that from our very first meeting I was impressed with Colby. He was thorough in everything he talked about. The club was underachieving and it was his priority to strengthen the squad for David Ward to do the rest. Over an hour or so he outlined the arrangements for accommodation, for a company car and, of course, the financial package. Basically, I was offered a signing-on fee and then a five-year contract of £20,000 a year plus bonuses, which could be anything from £300 for a first team win to £20 for an 'A' team appearance. All these figures were gross and liable to Income Tax and National Insurance, to be deducted before payment by the club. There was no firm promise of an automatic job and my request for it to be added to my contract was refused. Bernard explained why – nearly all league players at that time were semi-professional rather than full-time players – but said they would help with introductions and contacts. In the light of what had happened – or not happened – at Swansea and Cardiff it was probably better for me to hear a realistic, guarded statement like that than to be promised the earth on a shaking of hands and then be left feeling hopelessly let down.

My first impressions of David Ward were also favourable. Apparently he was the last Leeds captain to win a trophy of any significance and you could sense the determination in him that the glory days should return. Those first impressions were pretty accurate. Over the next year the support and advice he gave me were first-class. I knew before I went that it's not easy for a prop-forward to successfully switch codes and it certainly wouldn't be a swift transformation. Ward left me in no doubt about that but he emphasised that if I signed he would give me all the help he could. And as I sat and listened in that airport hotel, with hardly a penny to my name and brassed off with a succession of broken promises by union officials, I knew there and then that I was heading north.

At that point, so did Tony Clement. Both of us shook hands with Bernard Colby and we parted with the draft contracts for our solicitors to look over. We even did a dummy signing session for a photograph and within a couple of days the papers were carrying stories that I 'was expected to sign' for Leeds within days. What happened in those next few days only strengthened my resolve to go ahead with the league deal. The phone never stopped, usually with calls from people telling me to hang on, that something would turn up. Eventually I unplugged the phone but not before all sorts of promises had been made. I was training at the Welsh Institute of Sport, at Sophia Gardens, when two of Cardiff's back room staff, John Evans and Gwynne Griffiths, phoned. They informed me that the club was trying to set me up in a full-time job as a trainee manager at the Institute. I would be managing the weight training and fitness facilities, although there were a few minor sticking points to be ironed out.

The secretary of the WRU, Denis Evans, contacted me at home to say, 'Don't go', with another vague promise of a possible appointment to that elusive development officer post I had been enquiring about for months. He could not promise me the job, I would have to apply the same as any other person, and the likelihood of the job being sorted in May was remote. So what was he offering me to stay? NOTHING.

The national team coach John Ryan phoned to say that I was the future, the team would be built around me. A district representative, Gordon Williams, came to the house on behalf of the Union to ask me to stay. Stan Thomas, a wealthy benefactor at the club, said he was doing everything in his power to pull in his many business connections. And so it went on.

Matters came to a head on the following Saturday after Cardiff had beaten Llanelli in a Welsh Cup tie at the Arms Park. As I hadn't formally signed or, indeed, made any public statement about my intentions, I had turned out for the first team. In the bar afterwards there was a lot of talk about what I might or might not do. Clem had phoned me to say that he had changed his mind because his family was in Swansea and he felt he wasn't ready to make the break. I respected his decision and told him not to worry because whatever he did wouldn't affect my own signing for Leeds. Another fellow Lion from the previous year, Mike Hall, who had himself been up to look around St Helen's before deciding to stay put, told several of the Cardiff team that I wouldn't go. The time had come to inform the club.

I told Alan Phillips that I would be signing for Leeds the following week. He immediately asked why and I pointed out that as I had a mortgage to pay and no job I literally had no choice. At that point Alan exploded and seeing April alongside me said, 'What do you need money for – look at all the jewellery she's wearing!'

That was not very clever and things could have become very heated, but luckily Bob Norster was at hand. Although he was obviously very disappointed himself he used all his diplomatic skills to calm everybody down. April and I left the clubhouse soon afterwards and, given the position we were in at that particular time in our lives, we knew we had made the right decision.

Throughout all this difficult time I had kept my mother and father fully informed. Deep down I knew they were both very disappointed, not least because it would mean that April and I would be setting up a new home miles away from Aberdare. But that happens to many families. What Dad, in particular, found hard to accept was that I had been pushed into a corner from which there was only one way out. He did say that he always thought that one day I would try my hand at rugby league but he did not expect it to come so soon. On the other hand he said he didn't blame me and gave me his full support in doing what he called the right thing in the circumstances. As always his words meant everything to me and with them still ringing in my ears April and I flew up to Leeds to complete the formalities. From that moment on I thought not about the past and what I was leaving behind but the future and what the two of us, together, were embarking on in a new chapter in our lives. We were as positive as that.

The draft contract from Leeds had already been checked out for us and been given the all-clear. As well as my solicitor, the Warrington chairman, Peter Higham, had offered to have a look at it and was generous enough to say it was a good one and that I'd be a fool to turn it down. This was a spirit of co-operation between rival clubs that was new in my experience! Les Miles went up to Leeds with us and Bernard Colby showed us around and took us out to dinner. The next day would see the formal signing of my contract at a press conference. This immediately struck me as incredibly professional and very well organised compared to what I'd experienced in union. Colby gave me one piece of advice beforehand. 'Be positive,' he said. 'You're here because you want to be a success as a player for a big club – it's not all about money.'

He was so right. I couldn't deny that what had set me off on the road north were financial considerations. As the final weeks in South Wales had gone by I realised that what was also driving me was an underlying ambition, that same ambition that I had in youth rugby, that whatever I did in life I had to be a success. Bernard Colby was putting into words what I already knew. My thoughts returned to Richard Webster and that day I visited him, when he was totally broke; the day I was carried off against Scotland in 1989 and how quickly I was forgotten until I returned from injury.

The press conference went well and at one point I was asked whether I really wanted to play league and my answer was that I had always watched the game on television and I was a big supporter of St Helens! We flew back to South Wales that afternoon with arrangements in hand for me to return permanently the following week.

Later that evening I went into a fish-and-chip shop near home and while I was waiting to be served overheard the two assistants deep in conversation.'He's gone then,' said one, to which the other replied, 'No he hasn't,' and again, 'Yes he has,' at which point they looked up and shouted, 'Oh, my God, it's you!!'

Hanging in the front room of our home in Aberaman was a painting of me in my 1989 Lions' shirt, a gift from John and Mair, my in-laws. That evening April and I went into the front room to sit quietly and reflect on the day's events only to find the painting face down on the floor. The nail on which it had been hanging was still in the wall and the wire at the back of the picture was still intact!

Obviously there was no going back . . .

Now came the big hurdle, training and playing. The time scale in that first week meant that there would be only one evening's training before I played my first game. David Ward concentrated on the most basic of all league skills, playing the ball after a tackle. All the other new techniques, taking the ball up, running tall, running backwards, tackling high rather than low, off-loading not on the first or second but at the very earliest the third tackle – these would come later. For now I had to master, or attempt to master, what looked simple enough from the touch-line, going to ground and getting back on my feet to play the ball.

There was never any question of me going straight into the first team but it suited me down to the ground that my league debut would be in a reserve team game at Halifax. But that was no joy ride, either. 'Get the Welshman!' was soon drifting across the gluepot of a pitch as I came up against the first of many league hardmen. This one was Brendan Hill, a 28-year-old who was used to ruling his home roost. The scuffles started early on and by the tenth minute both Hill and our hooker Martin Smithson had been sent off. A couple more were despatched to the sin-bin and it really was a case of welcome to rugby league! But I lasted an hour before being substituted and we won the game 24–0. I was reasonably satisfied but totally exhausted. The alien nature of the game had taken its toll and I felt as though both my calves and hamstrings were about to burst due to the running backwards, something you don't do in rugby union. The real business would get under way in the weeks that followed and it was important to me that I earned the rest of the squad's respect and got to know them as quickly as possible.

In any club some personalities stand out and I soon became aware that at Headingley the coach, David Ward, was a Leeds man through and through. He had a real passion for the club and its history. I remember David taking both my parents and April's parents around the club to show them all the past players. He was always very emotional when talking about Leeds and it was he who resisted strongly the change in strip from the traditional hoops to the kind of league strip we see today. Ward was all-powerful because he was responsible for the tactics and for preparing every player for the victories that would not only gain league points but, equally important, earn cash bonuses. That was the bottom line and there was never going to be any problem with motivation. But he was also aware that if the results went against him every game was potentially his last.

Club captain, Gary Schofield, was another personality who sat at the top of the pile. Schofield had a big reputation as a player and was well established in the Great Britain team. He was an outside-half like no other I had come across so far in my career. He was heavily built with huge arms and was a big tackler. I found him friendly enough but spent very little time in his company. His favourite watering hole after matches was a pub called the Town Hall Tavern, run by an ex-Leeds player, where he and his clique would gather. They did invite me to join them though sometimes the accusation of being a union player who had come north for big bucks would rear its head. One very tiresome fact about rugby league players was the constant ribbing of rugby union players; that they were soft, while league players were much harder. A couple of months after my arrival one of Leeds ex-players Kevin Fox could not resist a joke about the RA-RA playing for Wales one minute and then being an A-team player at Leeds the next. Dave Heron was there and he politely advised Fox to back off as this was one RA-RA who would hit back. He also assured Fox that in his opinion he would come off second best to this RA-RA. This sort of incident was the exception rather than the rule. I soon had my own circle of friends.

Players like Heron and John Holmes had been coaxing me through my early games. Others such as Mike Kuiti and Gary Lord and their wives Sue and Debbie had made April and me feel very welcome. Mike was a tough Kiwi loose-forward with considerable ball skills and was a great organiser on the field. The former Wales centre Rob Ackerman had already been up north for four years and transferred to Leeds at about the time I arrived. He was a good bloke to have around – even though I still remembered that comment out in Canberra expressing the hope I wasn't like him! He took me under his wing when we played in the same games.

For my first two months we lived in a hotel but soon April and I found a place of our own. Everyone had made her feel very welcome which was a relief because she had given up a good position in Cardiff. Unknown to her, Wayne Phillips, her senior officer at Mid-Glamorgan County Council, had sent her qualifications to his counterpart in Leeds and after a few weeks on temporary contracts she was offered a permanent post as a training officer. Being April she threw herself into everything heart and soul and she wasn't homesick at all.

Two days after my initial run-out with the A-team David Ward had introduced me to first team rugby as a substitute in a cup match against Barrow. I was a big signing for the club and my first game would ensure a bigger than normal crowd.

Barrow were positioned at the bottom of the league and the 90 points' thrashing they received said it all. I had played over half an hour but after that another two months would go by whilst I served my apprenticeship with the reserves. Ward continued to take an active interest in me and always wanted me to train with the first team whenever A-team duties allowed. This was especially the case on Saturday mornings and then every Sunday he wanted me to attend the big game of the week if only to get a feel of what made the club tick.

'My name is on you,' he used to say, meaning that it was his responsibility to mould me into a top-flight league forward. Perhaps I was kidding myself but I had the impression that he liked my attitude. 'Run tall, you rugby union bastard!' was another of his more endearing phrases as I gradually got used to the idea that I couldn't carry the ball with my head down.

I had arrived in Leeds thinking that I was fit because I was streets ahead of most of the props I had come up against in union, David Sole apart. I soon discovered that though I was bigger than most opposite numbers in league I was also five yards slower. I knew my running fitness had to improve and I did endless 20-metre sprints to build up my dynamism over short distances.

What was really hard to get used to was the running backwards, as we faced up to the six carries from the attacking team. You were required to move forward as a line to put pressure on the ball carrier with the possibility of making a tackle, then retreat as quickly as possible to an on-side position before the opposition played the ball again. This would be repeated six times before a changeover unless the opposition were forced to make an error. There's a concrete path around the perimeter of the Headingley pitch and Ward set me a target of eight laps running backwards without stopping. I achieved that eventually – after eight months!

The priority was to become more agile, faster and above all a more powerful player to take on smaller opponents and also to develop the passing skills of a centre. The ball-in-play time was huge compared to what I had been used to. There were simply no rest periods as in every game you were constantly on the move. I soon learned, also, that a main part of a prop's duties was to take the ball on the first or second drive up field. Also when the other side were in possession of the ball to make the first or second tackle. In any one game I could expect to carry the ball at least 20 times and make up to 30 tackles – in Wales a union forward might on a good day make a dozen.

At the end of my first season, Ward told me that I had developed more quickly than expected and that he was excited by my prospects. That made me feel good.

7

MAKING THE GRADE

Dear Miss Thomas

. . . Quite frankly I am not interested in the reasons why David Young decided to go north. Nor am I interested in David Young's progress as a Rugby League player.

The point I was trying to make was that David Young gave away a career of exceptional promise in Rugby Union for a career of mediocrity in Rugby League. That is my opinion, that he made that decision for money is fact.

The other point I was trying to make was that I cannot recall a satisfactory transfer and transition by a Rugby Union prop forward to the Rugby League code.

Yours sincerely

D.P. Evans

The 'Miss Thomas' to whom this letter was addressed was April, four months before we were married in 1991, and 'D.P. Evans' was secretary of the Welsh Rugby Union. His sentiments are fairly clear and were written in reply to April's own letter following a television programme that considered why so many union players went north. The conclusion that Evans had reached in his interview was that it was a case of not so much fame as out-and-out fortune. Not very original, to say the least, but what was different about his contribution was that he labelled me a 'deserter' who had taken the big bucks and abandoned a system that had developed me for several years. There was also the suggestion that I was struggling to make the grade – and would go on struggling. Perhaps his comments were made off the cuff because once I had travelled north he was, I assume, totally unaware of any of the circumstances affecting my progress in rugby league.

This was the same Denis Evans, a paid employee, who, when the news broke that Leeds were about to sign me, had phoned to ask me to hang on for a few months without any income while the Welsh Rugby Union prepared to advertise jobs as development officers.

He had a point, of course, because I have never denied that finance was a major factor in my decision to sign for Leeds. But it was a case of money to pay the bills rather than a small fortune that would give me a life of luxury at the age of 22. Evans had known that when he had dangled the prospect of possible employment with the Union in front of me. My Aberaman neighbours had worked it out for themselves when I occasionally turned up in my club-sponsored car – a Lada Samara!

April accepted that he was entitled to his opinion but when watching the programme *Up North – Whose Grass is Greener?* at our home at Leeds, she strongly objected to his dismissive manner. Perhaps he was writing on behalf of the Union; I'll give him the benefit of the doubt. April asked Evans the question 'Is it possible with the exodus of so many Welsh stars that one day it would be possible to watch these players make up the nucleus of the Great Britain Rugby League side?' As it turned out most of them – Jonathan Davies, Mark Jones, Paul Moriarty and others – did go on to play for Great Britain. As for me, unfortunately my letter of selection came a little too late as it arrived just as arrangements were being finalised for my return to Cardiff in 1996. I was tempted because I would have answered a few critics but for me it was not meant to be. I do, however, have the letter to prove that I was to be considered for the Great Britain tour to Australia in October 1996.

I could point out that the previous year three top officers of the WRU had resigned after they had travelled unannounced to watch a rebel tour of South Africa. Now that really was a case of Monopoly money – a so-called World XV went there a few weeks after the 1989 Lions' tour to Australia during which several of the players were recruited – Robert Jones, Anthony Clement, Robert Norster amongst them I had also been made a very lucrative offer, in the region of £30,000, to tour with the World XV. My international career was then in its infancy stages and I was told that should I take up the offer it could have serious consequences on any future international caps. I did not want to threaten my future career so after taking advice from senior Welsh Rugby Union officials I declined the offer.

Anyway, Evans was clearly not impressed with April's account of my move to the north but what struck me about his letter was the tone of it.

I may or may not cut the mustard in rugby league but he certainly wasn't wishing me well. 'Nor am I interested in David Young's progress as a Rugby League player . . .' speaks for itself. More than anything I thought he was rubbishing me. It was attitudes like this that helped to drive me on. It is hard to believe now that barely four years later, the barriers between league and union would come down and there would be free traffic between the two codes.

But before that Evans had another very public falling-out with rugby league that did little to portray the Union in a good light.

By 1992 there were so many ex-union caps in the north that an attempt was made to resurrect a Wales Rugby League side. This was going to be quite a task. No national team had been selected for seven years but with Jonathan Davies, John Devereux, Allan Bateman and nearly a dozen others available to be slotted in with league thoroughbreds like Anthony Sullivan, a game was arranged with Papua New Guinea at the Vetch Field in Swansea. There was a lot of interest, particularly as the union team was going through a terrible patch. A crowd of 12,000 turned up and we won 68–0. So another game was fixed with France at the same venue. As luck would have it we were due to play on a Sunday and the day before Wales were playing Scotland in a Five Nations match at the Arms Park.

Nothing seemed more logical than for us to go along to the game to shout Wales on, after all there were several players who were to play that we were still friendly with. Our team manager Jim Mills requested tickets that we would, of course, pay for. Denis Evans came out of the woodwork again. 'We cannot arrange tickets for Rugby League players . . . there is no way I can justify that,' he said. This caused a huge furore in the press with one big league fan, the writer Colin Welland, denouncing the Welsh Rugby Union for practising what he considered apartheid. We never got our tickets and all 25 of us watched the union international on television in our hotel.

Several months later, April and I took some satisfaction when we read in the national paper that Evans had resigned under a cloud from his post at the WRU. Later, when he was fined for a driving offence, April suggested that we contact him to ask if we could buy his car! That I think was a measure of how much Evans's remarks had upset April at a time when we least needed it.

It was good to be part of a Wales team again and the excitement we caused by playing in South Wales and giving the fans a chance to see us was incredible. Over the next three years we played seven matches in

Swansea and Cardiff, always at soccer grounds, which would eventually lead to an even more high-profile stage, a rugby league World Cup. But that was still in the future – the bread-and-butter of my career was making the grade at club level and that was certainly not all sweetness and light. Despite the encouraging noises made by David Ward my progress at Leeds was not all that I had hoped it might be. Now it might surprise people like Denis Evans that for me, it was not a case of being there, playing second-team rugby and occasionally in the top side, and still picking up the cash; that was never going to be enough.

After 18 months at Headingley I had only played eight first-team games. I could have gone through the motions and adopted a laid-back attitude. After all, April and I had set up a lovely home near Carnegie College in the city. I had a very promising job with Project Vehicle Management that was similar to my earlier work with Jordan's in South Wales – but this was a thriving and well-established company with long-term prospects for me. But to accept what I had off the field and let my playing side slip would have been a betrayal of everything my family and I had striven for since I was a kid. I could have made a case for throwing in the towel after a period when nothing seemed to be going in my favour.

I had actually managed a couple of games for the first team but then picked up a bad ear injury that required plastic surgery. It was a pure accident. I had positioned myself for a tackle when the attacker's knee caught my ear, tearing it from the side of my head. This came at a particularly bad time as I felt I was in with a real chance of breaking into the first team on a regular basis. When I did fight back to match fitness I was banned for two games and fined £200 out of my own pocket after being sent off in an A-team match. Even one year after I had switched codes I was still the so-called ex-union star being targeted by some of the hard boys of second-team rugby – and I wasn't prepared to take things lying down.

No sooner had I come back from my suspension than I was sent off again at Hull and this time I was out of pocket to the tune of £400 and, worse still, banned for six weeks. The great irony was that both first-team props, Roy Powell and Paul Dixon, were out injured and the door to the first team was wide open. Instead, I had to kick my heels whilst I served my suspension and could only watch helplessly as the club signed two more props, Shaun Wane and Steve Molloy, to plug the gaps. This meant that when we were all fit and available I would now be one of five, not three as previously, competing for two places.

The time had come to be realistic. Was the cup half-empty or half-full? Sadly, I came to the conclusion that it was a case of the former. David Ward was under pressure himself as the team was still not winning regularly in a league dominated by Wigan RLFC. He seemed reluctant to play me regularly which I felt would have helped me to develop a lot more quickly. He preferred to stick with the tried and tested league products. The last straw came when I actually played for the firsts against Bradford and won the man-of-the-match award – only to be dropped again for the next game.

I knew that I would be up against it for Leeds just to agree to release me. I was one of the biggest signings for the club and there would be a lot of egg on their faces if they were to let me go without any notable success. Every rugby league club is operated as a business; the account sheets have to be balanced. I knew that Leeds would need to recover some of the money that had been spent on me. Any transfer fee would seriously affect my chances of a transfer to another club. Rugby league is like any other sport – there are rich clubs and there are poor clubs, and Leeds are one of the richest. There were not many clubs in the first division who could afford a transfer fee, but would Leeds let me go for nothing?

A meeting was arranged with the club's chief executive, Alf Davies, and Ward at which I left them in no doubt that I was unhappy with the lack of opportunities coming my way. There were rumours flying around that Warrington and Salford were interested in me but Ward's response was that I should be patient and the chances would come. The saga dragged on for a few weeks and I met again with Alf Davies and with the secretary Bill Carter. There was no point in Ward being present because he wasn't prepared, at that stage at least, to give any consideration to my leaving. I suspect that deep down he realised that if I went it would reflect badly on his coaching and development of a big money signing. If so, he would have been right. In all my time at Leeds, Ward never gave me one-to-one coaching or any technical analysis. I went on record as saying I had never been coached as an individual at all – and I meant it.

Davies and Carter at least agreed to let me go in principle – but at a price. They put a transfer fee on my head and even though I didn't know what it was I suspected it was too high and prospective clubs would turn away. Luckily, a knight in shining armour in the shape of Kevin Tamati appeared on the horizon. I had impressed him when I had played against him several weeks before and he had realised that there was talent which needed to be tapped into – Kevin was now coach of Salford. He took the view that an ex-Lions' prop Leeds had thought enough of 18 months before to sign for a healthy fee must have some potential. So another drawn-out set of transfer talks began.

This gave me a bit of time to take stock of the situation. There were definitely pluses and minuses. April and I had settled down in Leeds and were about to be married and could certainly do without another unnecessary upheaval. The club had not written me off completely. In fact, with the help of Robert Ackerman and Dean and Clayton Bell arrangements had been almost finalised for me to spend the summer in New Zealand playing league for Papa Newi in the Auckland area. The team was coached by Frank Endicott who later coached New Zealand and travelled to Britain to coach Wigan RLFC. This could only be good for my development. But what would I return to the following season? More A-team rugby? There was no escaping the five-into-two-won't-go equation with the club's props and the Leeds board was obviously taking the view that at £20,000 a year I was an expensive commodity as a reserve team player.

From the outset Salford, being one of the poorer teams, made it plain that they couldn't match that basic wage even if I played for their first team. The best they could come up with was £15,000 so was I prepared to take a pay cut? The answer had to be 'Yes' as my chances of breaking through into the big time in club rugby would be increased considerably. Satisfaction that I was realising my potential was always far more important than the money.

I had to remember though, that I was turning my back on a big club, staffed with, by this time, full-time professionals on and off the field – a club with excellent facilities and a big supporter base – to become part of a much smaller operation run by part-timers and few, if any, big-name players. If I joined Salford I would have to make a real success of it as soon as possible. To be sidelined there as I had been at Leeds would mean me waving good-bye to any long-term league career.

Somehow I knew my future lay at Salford but with three years of my contract with Leeds still to run there was still some hard bargaining to be done. One of their senior players, John Holmes, advised me that I would be crazy to walk away from Headingley without a settlement fee so I went back to them to begin another month of haggling. My trump card, if I had one at all, was that I knew they were desperate to reduce their financial commitment. Eventually we agreed on a settlement, and in the circumstances, it was an amicable parting.

My projected summer in New Zealand and possible honeymoon for myself and April was called off as Salford wanted me for pre-season training. That suited me down to the ground and I threw myself into my new work. There were no full-time players at the club so I kept my job with PVM in Leeds and, for the time being at least, we made no plans to move house. I soon discovered that driving across the M62 three or four times a week in winter was not to be taken lightly. If I was going to give 100 per cent commitment to Salford I would have to move to Manchester. That would be no hardship as it was a happy club with no cliques and a determination to become a force in the game again. It had gone through a glamorous period 20 years before when the Wales and Lions' fly-half David Watkins had signed for them, quickly followed by Maurice Richards, Keith Fielding and Mike Coulman; and Friday-night rugby at their ground, The Willows, was the place to be seen. But that was history and it was now a struggle to hold their own alongside the giants of the modern game.

We put our house in Leeds on the market and started to look for a new home in Manchester. The move had to be put on hold, however, for April and I to be married. The ceremony took place at a very old Welsh chapel, Siloa, in Aberdare, on 27 May 1991. It was a quiet affair but we tried to ensure that all our friends from union and league were there, and they all were except for Sue and Mike Kuiti. They had travelled back to New Zealand for the imminent birth of their first son, Jordan.

We were married at 2 p.m. and the reception was held at the Ty Newydd Country Hotel, Hirwaun. The service itself was unique. We had a very, very old minister called Mr Davies. I thought from the outset that he spoke very slowly and he said only one or two words at a time for me to repeat after him. He asked April how she was known, April or Michelle? After being told that she was known as April he called her Michelle all the way through the ceremony. I remember hearing April's elderly nan shouting 'Her name is April!'.

Paul Moriarty said that all he remembers seeing at the service were several very large sets of shoulders shaking as guests tried to stifle their laughter. Later at the reception Robert Ackerman (remember him? – 'Oh no. Not Ackerman!'), who was my best man told me that he had informed the minister that I was extremely nervous and as I did not wish to spoil the service would it be possible for the wedding vows to be taken very slowly. The thought of playing in front of a very large stadium full to capacity did not frighten me but the thought of saying my vows in front of April's elderly grandparents had absolutely terrified me.

The speeches were got out of the way and pretty soon the fun started. April and I noticed that the centre table flower arrangements had started to disappear and we soon realised that the friendly rivalry between union and league was developing into a full blown competition. Who could eat the most flowers from the arrangements? Pretty soon there were pairs of players doing sit-ups, press-ups, press-ups with several people on the back, handstands, you name it. It was all good entertainment, especially for the oldies, some of whom had never seen anything like it. But the best was yet to come.

We had ordered a buffet to be served at 9 p.m. but when the families ventured to fetch some food they found empty trays. The players had ravaged the lot. The caterers, however, were very understanding and quickly made more for the families.

I think that several of the guests regretted their actions the next day when the hangovers kicked in. One of these was Richard Webster who was seen walking through the grounds looking for his false tooth. Apparently it had fallen out sometime during the evening when he was reportedly being sick.

Back in Manchester, I soon felt that I was making real progress under the direction of Kevin Tamati. He was not everyone's cup of tea and as time went on I became aware of a real issue between him and the board, concerning his commitment to the club. He worked for Warrington Council and there was a feeling that he wasn't giving enough time, particularly in terms of preparation, to training sessions. I had no complaints on that score because for me, at that stage in my career, Tamati was the perfect mentor. He was an international prop in his own right and had achieved some notoriety for a punch-up with an Australian prop that had continued after the two of them had been sent off.

As a coach he was remarkably laid-back, though with me I think he realised that if he could make me into an automatic first-teamer he would win a few Brownie points. I received plenty of advice. He taught me that instead of running straight at tacklers I should be looking for the gaps and to do this I should also be varying my angles of running. My tackle count averaged 32–38 a match and on several occasions topped the 40 mark. On one occasion I had broken the club record, completing 54 tackles in one game.

Tamati stressed that what I needed more than anything was regular rugby and this was music to my ears. He gave me the opportunities I had been looking for over the previous year and there was no doubt that my all-round game was sharpened up considerably. I made a bit of an impression on my debut, an annual pre-season friendly against Swinton. I won the man-of-the-match award. Travelling home with April across the M62 I remember feeling that my rugby league career was well and truly back on track. The day was made even more complete when April announced that we were expecting our first child. I went to bed that night floating on air. Everything at last seemed to be going in the right direction in that first season at The Willows. I never looked back.

As a team, however, we were never going to win top honours. We had several useful performers, including my old Cardiff and Wales team-mate Adrian Hadley on the wing and Steve Gibson, a tall full-back from Brisbane. The half-backs were Steve Kerry and Peter Williams, who had played for England when I won my first cap for Wales in the 1987 World Cup quarter-final. We were good enough to sustain a comfortable mid-table position in the league.

I finished my first season at Salford with a great feeling of anticipation and I was definitely looking forward to the second. Firstly though there was some unfinished business at the maternity ward, Prince Charles Hospital. On 18 May 1992 at 7.59 a.m. Thomas-Rhys was delivered weighing in at nearly 9lbs – my first son. It was one of the proudest moments of my life and made me more determined than ever to be a success.

Our second season at Salford started with some notable victories. We defeated clubs such as Halifax, losing narrowly to St Helens. By the time winter came around we were expecting our second child and I was made club captain. That was a sign that my ambitions as a player were reaching fruition but it also brought me into closer contact with the unpleasant world of club politics.

It soon became apparent that Kevin Tamati's days as Salford coach were numbered. His day job was taking up more and more time and the results were worsening. We lost by 70 points away to Wigan and on the following Monday Tamati didn't turn up to take a training session. The knives were out. The players and the fans had already made their dissatisfaction known to the board and without further hesitation the chairman, John Wilkinson, sacked him. But it was suspected that a replacement had already been lined up.

Garry Jack was a top-notch full-back from Balmain who had played over 20 tests for Australia, and he had won the highest award for rugby league players, the Golden Boot. In Salford terms he was a major signing though there were the inevitable mutterings in the dressing-room. Our regular full-back, Steve Gibson, knew he could wave goodbye to his place in the team. Garry Jack was a true professional and soon made his presence felt, for the better. He was more business-like than anyone who had gone before, with outstanding preparation for every training session and the introduction of new moves and plays. Nowadays, pre-match analysis of the opposition is common-place, even in rugby union, but in 1994 it was almost unheard of. Jack would provide us with an overview of our next opponents. He would provide a breakdown of components of opponents' games into 'Marker Play', 'Kicking Game' and 'General Play'.

As an example, when we played St Helens that season, he began his analysis with the following: 'St Helens like to promote the ball wherever and whenever they can. They play with a lot of RISK and they are good at doing this so we must defend aggressively and wrap up the ball.

'They will build to their right-hand side then spread it back to Loughlin and Joynt out wide. Our right-hand side defence – Andy Burgess, Bob and Critch – nominate your man and be in position. You must tackle them around the chest area, smash them in defence. Low tackles promote the ball, especially on Neil and Dannant up front.

'GOOD DEFENCE WILL ALWAYS BEAT GOOD ATTACK.'

And so it went on, highlighting the strengths and weaknesses of different players in the Saints' line-up and what our own plays would be. These would include 'Quick play the ball . . . David and Ged doing the hits . . . For the first 15 minutes don't give them the soft option by spreading the ball early on . . .Take it to them.'

The conclusion would be: 'CONTROL THE BALL AND WE CONTROL THE GAME. THEY DON'T LIKE PRESSURE – DOMINATE IN DEFENCE.'

The effect of these methods was not startling but the team undoubtedly became more consistent. Jack had said at the beginning of his reign that if we could keep our points difference low then we would eventually move up the ladder. We lost our first four games and ended up middle table with a points difference of five. But like everyone Jack had a weakness. He was blinkered. He concerned himself only with a single group of 20 players. Players that he thought would deliver success. In some ways it is hard to argue with that because he would be judged on promotions and championships. In any sport it seems that success must come immediately, there never seems to be time for steady development. He did not seem concerned with the development of the youngsters at the club and these were left to languish in the A-team. An interesting test-case of his overall player development skills came to the fore when a new rugby union signing joined us.

My past was catching up with me because the new face was none other than Richard Webster. My old sparring-mate whose career had gone side-by-side with my own through Wales Youth, the summer in Canberra, the first caps in the World Cup and club rugby with Swansea, had continued to make a name for himself in the three years since I had left South Wales. Despite six knee operations Webby had won thirteen caps for Wales and had been a Lion in New Zealand in 1993. Although he didn't play in the tests out there he was a mainstay of the mid-week side and had shamed several others with his 150 per cent effort and commitment and had won many new admirers. Now he was about to follow the same road north. Salford's scouts in South Wales had approached him and my only input, when asked, was to tell the club that they would be getting someone who would put his body on the line and never shirk from hard work. Webby would make his own decision but on a visit to look around the club and the area he stayed with us overnight. It gave us the chance to catch up on all the gossip from back home and we were able to introduce him to our increasing family, which by now had grown. Thomas-Rhys, although still a baby himself, now had a baby brother, Lewis David, born 5 August 1993.

All I told Webby was that Salford was an honest club that valued people who did their best and that it was up to him to decide whether the financial package on offer met his needs. Without further discussion he returned to Swansea but two weeks later Richard Webster was a Salford player. He arrived in the middle of Jack's first season and all was going well. The coach had brought in an assistant, Howard Cartwright, and there was a good deal of time spent on skills. With a few victories under their belt the team had come around to supporting the new regime but a month after Webby arrived the next recruit was to seriously threaten the sweet harmony of everything that Garry Jack was trying to achieve.

The signing of Andy Gregory was trumpeted far and wide as 'the bargain of the season'. It was hard to argue with that assessment for Greg was a league legend and with him added to the team our upward climb continued. He was a great player who had done the business for

Warrington, Wigan and Leeds. He had the reputation as a troublemaker, however, and unfortunately this reputation seemed to precede him. I got on with him as a player, though, and he was great company when having a quiet pint. He was a humorous man with loads of stories to relate to anyone who would listen; but my gut feeling from day one was that he would never be satisfied with being merely a team player. He had achieved everything in the game and I felt that he would never be happy playing second fiddle to anyone; he liked to call the shots. I kept my feelings to myself but it was always in the back of my mind that Greg might do anything to get his own way.

At first, Jack was excited by Gregory's arrival, his assessment being that such a class half-back would inevitably improve performances.

'What do you think?' asked Garry of me.

I had a great deal of respect for Garry and did not wish to see him fall into a trap, but he was so naïve. It had not occurred to him that a player like Greg who was obviously in the twilight years of his career would want to proceed into coaching when it was time for him to hang up his boots just as he, himself, had done.

'I think you may have just lost your job!' was my reply.

He didn't see it at first but as the months went by Gregory became very active behind the scenes and the writing was soon on the wall. Greg was very clever. He started by winning the players' favour. He had many contacts in the sporting and entertainment fraternity of the north-west and we would be taken to watch Manchester City regularly and occasionally he even arranged training sessions at Man United's complex, the Cliff. That was the first phase. The next was to start criticising the coach's methods behind his back. Several of the squad who felt they hadn't been getting a fair deal from him, especially Richard Webster, Jason Critchley, Phil Ford and Mark Lee, fell for it. When the defeats came, as sooner or later they would, the knife really went in and Gregory laid the blame firmly at Jack's door.

Sensing that there was something going on, without quite being able to put his finger on it, Jack confronted Gregory only to be assured that there was no problem. But meanwhile Gregory was going from strength to strength in the eyes of the board. There was no denying that he had business contacts and eventually he made the introductions that brought one or two sponsors to the club. One particular sponsor supplied us with an electric score board making us the envy of several other clubs. Jack made a fatal mistake when he replaced Howard Cartwright with Gregory as his assistant. Talk about signing your own death warrant! It had been a genuine attempt to bring Greg on-side but it backfired spectacularly.

As captain I had tended to keep my distance from Gregory and he adopted much the same approach with me but now he was assistant coach we had more contact. Eventually he asked me to call the players to a meeting to discuss the coach's position. This was a new scenario altogether and I refused point blank, saying that I would speak to Garry privately. That wasn't good enough for him. Greg chose a player, Mark Lee, to call the meeting instead. Mark had been first choice hooker until the arrival of Jack and after the club had signed Peter Edwards as hooker his first-team games became limited to bench appearances. I had no option other than to go along and hear what was said and it wasn't very pleasant. Several players criticised the coach and again they looked to me to take it further. I told them there was absolutely no question of taking the matter to the board behind Garry's back. I had listened to the points being raised at the meeting and although I did agree with one or two they were very minor in my opinion. At the conclusion of the meeting, I said I would speak to Garry personally, which is what I did.

Unfortunately that achieved very little because Garry Jack could not accept any of the perceived faults. He ignored my advice to do something, or at least to be seen to do something. Events then overtook him rapidly. We lost heavily at home to Castleford and there was a noisy demonstration at the ground by disgruntled fans. That was fertile territory for Gregory and when I refused another players' meeting the matter went straight to the board.

A second meeting was called which was supposed to be players only. Greg had, I believe, refused to attend the meeting, as he knew that he had something to gain from it, if it went the way he hoped. I attended in my capacity as captain. On arriving at the club I parked my car in the usual place but sat for a brief moment to see Greg talking to players outside the club before they entered the meeting. It occurred to me that he was perhaps briefing them before the meeting had even started; an action that I condemned him for. The meeting started and before long it was suggested that someone should call the chairman so that the players could put their views to him. Sitting at the back of the room I refused, and Mark Lee was elected to telephone the chairman. It was the view that this needed to be sorted out as soon as possible. Mark Lee returned to the meeting only to say that John Wilkinson, the chairman, was already on his way and accompanied by Albert White, Greg's close friend on the board. Both entered the room and immediately started asking individuals their views. I made it clear that I disagreed with the consensus and that I did not want to be a party to this underhanded way of dealing with things. I have always been honest and say what I think to people's faces and never behind their backs. It did occur to me in the car on the way home that this could possibly have been a set-up by Greg and that everyone at the club had fallen hook, line and sinker for it. My protests went unheeded and Garry Jack was sacked almost immediately. It was a sad end for a great player.

There was fall-out for April and me. We were good friends of Garry and Donna Jack but while I was heading for France to play in an international for Wales, they phoned April and laid the blame for the dismissal firmly at my door. We were both very upset, April particularly so – she had just learned that she was expecting our third child and was at the time quite ill. I had to return the call to the Jacks from the airport to tell them that they were barking up the wrong tree.

On my return from France I arranged to meet with Garry as I wanted to put the record straight. By this time though it had become apparent from several members of the board that my involvement with the meeting had been minimal and that I had tried to do everything possible to stop the events that had occurred. But Garry had been left with a very bitter taste in his mouth and there was no going back. He had even fallen out with Graham McCarthy, the Salford secretary with whom he had been friendly for years. The Jacks decided to return to Australia, and they packed their bags and left England a couple of weeks later but thankfully our friendship was still intact. This made both of us feel at least a little better but back at the Salford club the fun and games were really about to start.

Andy Gregory had asked me to stay on as captain and although I wasn't at all happy with the change of coach the fact remained that I was still the players' choice and, being professional, that was something I had to respect. So I carried on – and we promptly lost our first home game of the Gregory regime 8–42 to Wigan. That could just about be explained away against the mighty Wigan but the situation at training sessions gradually deteriorated.

The initial excitement by certain senior players soon evaporated. Steve Hampson, a close friend of Greg's from his Wigan days, was one of the first to go as did Phil Ford, who did not fear anyone, and Sam Panapa, all of whom had been enthusiastic supporters of Greg a few months before.

These were all seasoned professionals who knew their way about and would certainly stand up to Greg when the going became tough. I felt quite strongly that they were seen as a threat and as they had served their purpose, as soon as their contracts ran out they were banished to other clubs. His coaching staff was changed completely, making sure that he was surrounded by people who were not a threat to his reign.

What often happened at training bordered on the disgraceful. Gregory was fond of a pint or two and it seemed at times when he turned up for training after a liquid lunch, he had nothing prepared for the session. There was one ridiculous situation when he said that his aim was to increase our stamina so that we could run in Indian file for 60 minutes non-stop instead of the usual 20 minutes. Progress was the word that he used. Skills training went out of the window and the only link with his predecessor was that he kept all of Garry Jack's set moves and plays. He and I worked together but at arm's length, outwardly supportive of one another. Beneath the surface, though, there was a feeling of resentment: on his part because he knew that I would stand up to him if things got out of hand; on my part because I knew that it would not be long before he decided that enough was enough and it would be my turn to take the flak.

Several years on as Greg's story unfolded and the man confessed to being an alcoholic I realised that he did indeed have problems during his time at Salford. He struggled to come to terms with the fact that once he had finished playing unless he made his name in coaching he would fade into the background. This may have contributed to his downfall. I am happy to see that now he appears to be on the way up once more.

On the field nothing spectacular happened in what was left of the 1994–95 season after Gregory took over. The great changes were taking place elsewhere in the rugby league world. The Australian millionaire Rupert Murdoch had bankrolled an entirely new structure at the top of the game that was to become known as Super League – but at a price. The game for the top clubs would move to the summer months, taking it away from direct competition with soccer and rugby union, and would be totally professional.

It was certainly an exciting new concept as along with the money that Murdoch invested came a Sky Television deal that would give Super League a shop window and also heralded a new age of razzmatazz. For Super League was all about entertainment. It was not to everyone's taste, certainly not the pie and a pint diehards, but it was unashamedly aimed at attracting a whole new generation of fans and investors. Rugby league is a great game but, whatever its champions pretend to the contrary, it remains a small one, still played within limited boundaries such as the north of England and Australia, with pockets of activity in New Zealand, France and outposts like Papua New Guinea.

There is nothing wrong with that and what Super League did was maximise its potential at club level. To go to a top-class league match these days and soak up the pre-match entertainment is an experience that all the family looks forward to. I know because my three boys were enthralled when April and I took them to Bradford's Valley Parade ground in summer 2001 to watch Bradford beat Wigan in an enthralling match. It has to be understood that today rugby league comes with a full entertainment package and all clubs have had to change in order to keep up with the top clubs. If there is a full house at every game the revenue from gate receipts, sale of merchandise etc. is all ploughed back into the club and the team.

But in 1995 Salford missed out. As with all new structures created almost overnight there were winners and losers. The first year of Super League meant that the bottom four teams in the top division would stay where they were, in a semi-professional winter sport, whilst the rest were creamed off into the bright new world of Murdoch's millions. As Salford looked on, Wigan, St Helens, Leeds and the other big clubs disappeared over the horizon. We were very disappointed to be playing in Division One and some were highly critical of John Wilkinson, chairman of Salford RLFC. Had he tried hard enough and spent enough money to keep us in the top flight? I do not know the answer to those questions but what I do know is that as the longest serving chairman in rugby league his loyalty to Salford cannot be questioned.

During one month in particular, prior to any plans being finalised, he took tremendous flak for even considering a merger between Salford and Oldham; a merger which could be likened perhaps to say a merger between Neath and Swansea. At one game there were fans parading banners with messages spelling out in no uncertain terms what they thought of the plan. In the end Wilkinson stuck his neck out. But what we faced was a winter campaign in a new First Division, similar in stature to soccer's Nationwide League these days, with the incentive of rejoining the elite clubs if we became champions. As a team we felt disappointed to be playing outside the top flight but as always I was supported from the stand by April and our three sons who at this time were aged three years, two years and six days. Owen James was born 14 September 1995. In May

1996 Salford did indeed become champions and that set up the renamed Salford Reds to dine at the top table in the summers that followed.

The changes in professional rugby, however, were not confined to the 13-a-side code. To nearly everyone's astonishment, the union game had also opened its doors to professionalism in September 1995 and that was to have an effect on my future at Salford.

8

GOING SOUTH

It was a situation I had never bargained for. My move north in 1990 had been one-way. My destiny lay in Leeds and then Manchester. But the whole future of rugby union as an amateur game run by blazered committee-men was under threat in 1995. First there was the blind ambition of Kerry Packer. What his fellow-countryman Rupert Murdoch had done in rugby league, he intended to do in rugby union. The two were arch-rivals and as Murdoch was finalising Super League, Packer was devising an even more audacious plan in union. A world rugby circus would sign up all the top players and contract them to a global competition that would take the game into a new age just as Packer had done with cricket in the 1970s. It was quite an idea but I took only a passing interest. Until, that was, a senior member of the current Wales team arrived in Manchester and arranged to see Richard Webster and me.

The proposition put to us was simple enough. Sign up with Packer and our league contracts would be paid off. Four teams were being put together in the UK – and they really were being put together because most of the existing Five Nations squads had already signed – and we would be playing against New Zealand, Australia and France for big money. The All Blacks, to a man, were already on board. The sticking point was the Springboks. After 20 years of sporting isolation they were at last back in the fold and they weren't about to give it up for a bit of cash. The cynic might argue that South African rugby had never been exactly short of a few million rand in the years when rebel tours visited their shores. Anyway South Africa was about to host the World Cup and nothing was to come in the way of that.

Webby and I were assured that with or without South Africa Packer's grand plan would go ahead and we committed ourselves to joining all the others who would change the face of rugby union forever. It had not been a one-way ticket after all. The next twist in the tail was that even as Packer and his men were within a couple of phone calls of total revolution, the union authorities trumped them.

In September 1995 the International Rugby Board announced that the game had gone 'open'.

At that point I didn't consider the implications for myself. I had already agreed an extension of my contract with Salford that would take me to 1997. Although there was speculation that was almost frenzied in South Wales about all the former stars returning to the union fold, I resisted the temptation to day-dream about playing again at Cardiff Arms Park.

Then came a phone call from Gareth Davies at Cardiff Rugby Club. My old club had been the first to prepare the groundwork for the new age and Gareth, a great player in his own right who had also been very successful in business and the media, had already been appointed as its first-ever chief executive.

'Are you interested in coming back to us?' was his fateful question.

Interested? Of course I was, I was a professional and open to offers! If my time in rugby league had taught me anything it was that you are a commodity in a limited market and if at any particular time you are being sought after you make the most of it. Jonathan Davies had already left league and was returning not to Llanelli but Cardiff. Not surprisingly that had attracted a blaze of publicity, though I couldn't help wondering whether Jiffy was putting his head on the block. All the expectations of Welsh rugby were being heaped on his shoulders. Could Wales, who apart from one successful season in 1994 had endured a disastrous six or seven years at international level and been turfed out of two World Cups before the quarter-finals, become world-beaters again? Could Jiffy and the rest of us lead them to the promised land?

There was a little doubt at the back of my mind and I told Gareth that in practical terms I was unavailable because of my Salford contract. On the other hand, I knew that Andy Gregory would love to see me go. The board would probably not be so accommodating. The chairman, John Wilkinson, admitted that he thought the writing was on the wall, that Salford and other league clubs would come under a lot of pressure to negotiate the release of several Welsh players but, for the time being at least, I was staying in Salford.

He wanted me to stay at Salford – at this time I was playing out of my skin and my name was being linked with selection for the forthcoming tour with Great Britain. At the same time he realised that my earning potential was being limited while staying at Salford as he was aware of offers being made to other players. He suggested that in order to keep everyone happy I might consider a winter out-of-season contract with Sale Rugby Union. There had already been discussions with both clubs about a possible ground share. Sale had been looking to move to another ground and felt that The Willows was the ideal place. The chairman saw me as the link between the two although he was quick to point out that Salford would still hold my registration.

It was an interesting idea. Sale had apparently agreed in principle to a lease agreement for my services throughout their season. Perhaps I should have been more opposed to being used as a pawn in what was a potentially good financial set-up for them but carried the distinct risk of burn-out for myself. I may have been a little naïve in thinking that as club captain I should expect to be used this way.

As it happened, nothing came of the master plan although it was precariously close to completion. Personal ego scuppered it after some of Sale's officials turned up at The Willows unannounced to look over the facilities and discuss changes. John Wilkinson more or less threw his toys out of the pram. It must be understood that John considered The Willows his baby. He had resurrected it from the ashes and had built it up into a very successful entertainment club. It was not just a rugby ground but a variety club regularly playing host to well known celebrities, a restaurant with a good reputation and a bar which was always full. I went to see Wilkinson and could hardly believe what I was hearing when he said, 'This is *my* club, not Sale's and they don't come here without me knowing about it!' On such little things do major business deals collapse.

However, Wilkinson had a Plan B up his sleeve. The other first-class union club in the area, Orrell, had also declared an interest. Our former fly-half Peter Williams was their rugby director and, again, the discussions moved quite quickly. This was all very unsettling for me, not to mention April. Approaches had been made by clubs from London but we felt that these would not represent a final move. Any move now had to be final, so these offers, although flattering, were not options we were prepared to consider. This meant that it was either stay put in Manchester where we were extremely happy, and play for a local club or move back to Wales and play for a Welsh club. The Cardiff factor hadn't gone away, either.

Gareth Davies had phoned a second time to say that an offer was being put together at his end. When I told him that I was on the verge of signing for Sale he had said, 'Don't do anything!' Then the Cardiff trail went cold.

Enter Swansea – after eight years. This was becoming ridiculous. To be serious, it wasn't ridiculous. There had been so much speculation and so many on-off deals flying around that I was coming to realise that a return to Wales was becoming more likely by the day. April had been marvellously understanding and had not put pressure on me to either stay or go. Her role, as always, was to be an equal partner where we discussed the options and weighed them up but we now had a family of three young sons to consider. We couldn't deny that the pull of Wales was becoming ever stronger. After all, this was an unexpected opportunity to return to our roots. As the possibility became a reality April was excited at the prospect of having the support not only of my family but hers also.

Cardiff had not been in touch for nearly a month so it was time to talk to Swansea. Mike Ruddock was coaching their team and I had an enormous respect for him. He had spoken to me briefly when I was in Swansea for the Rugby League World Cup and I knew that he and I were on the same wavelength. April and I drove down the motorway and met Geoff Atherton and a couple of other Swansea officials near Ross-on-Wye. It was a friendly meeting but I could see that a deal was unlikely. In the first flush of professional rugby union the Welsh Rugby Union were brokering players' contracts. The national squad members would be appointed as development officers and would be paid a retainer. There would be separate club contracts. That sounded simple enough but it didn't stack up – Swansea were proposing to pay me £40,000 but if the WRU came in with a £30,000 retainer then Swansea would reduce their input to £10,000. They were effectively putting a salary 'cap' of £40,000 on my head. I had prior knowledge of the retainer and knew that this was almost inevitable. I couldn't agree to that and so the negotiations broke down there and then. They also offered a sponsored car, a Micra. I couldn't even imagine myself driving one because it would be impossible for me to fit into it!

Prior to my meeting with Swansea I had been contacted by the WRU's director of rugby, Terry Cobner. He told me that he was working hard to get me back into a Welsh club and there was a development officer's post in the pipeline that would be worth £30,000 a year. That brought a smile to my face. I appreciated that Cobner was trying to do his best. He had been out of the often stifling Welsh rugby environment himself for a few years and now he was back there trying to change things from within. He has always been supportive of me and has delivered on everything he promised. I couldn't forget, though, that another one of those elusive development officer's jobs had been dangled in front of me in an effort to keep me in Wales in 1990. It had been worthless then; this time, possibly, it might have more substance.

All things considered, it looked as if I would be staying in league after all until yet another call came from Cardiff. This time I told Gareth Davies that I was annoyed. When I had left the club all those years before it had been a case of promises, promises, promises. Had anything changed? By this time April was becoming increasingly concerned about the children – they were fast approaching the summer break and we did not know what was happening. I think subconsciously she hoped that we would stay in Manchester because after all it was the only place our children had ever known and staying put would mean less disruption for them.

But the answer came that it *had* changed and changed for the better. The club chairman was now Peter Thomas, a local businessman who was in the throes of reorganising the club as a plc. Comparisons are often drawn between Peter and the millionaires who threw themselves into English clubs like Newcastle, Richmond and Wasps at that time. That is entirely unfair as well as incredibly inaccurate. Unlike them, Peter Thomas is a rugby man through and through. He played for Cardiff in the 1960s, and is hugely ambitious for the future of his local club.

Two days after I had voiced my displeasure to Gareth Davies, Peter Thomas was on the phone. He got straight to the point, 'Do you want to come to Cardiff?' I told him that although I was cheesed-off with the way everything seemed to be going around in circles the answer had to be 'Yes'.

His response was refreshingly forthright: 'It will be sorted.'

I had to admire Peter's next move. He sent his special envoy to meet John Wilkinson at Salford – Jonathan Davies. There could be no better man to arrive at a rugby league club's door to put the case for union. Jiffy was a legend in both codes and he did the business. The only proviso made by Salford was that I had to see out the 1996 Super League season with them and return to Cardiff in September. We finally knew where our future was.

But it was not as straightforward as it sounded. I had been carrying a serious ankle injury for several weeks. Salford, in a cost-cutting exercise, had refused to get me a scan. In rugby league every penny counts and if a player can carry on with an injection then so be it. Ask Adrian Hadley who played for several weeks with ankle ligament damage before being sent to Lilleshall for rehabilitation. Greg had virtually begged me to carry on playing because the team needed a leader – by this time I had led Salford for four seasons. I carried on, having pain-killing injections, but as each game went on I played less and less. Sixty minutes became 55 minutes became 40 minutes until one day I decided enough was enough, I could not carry on any more. In one of the last games I played I was on the field for only 20 minutes. It was time for something to be done.

The fact that I had been playing with pain-killing injections had only served to make the injury more serious and a scan revealed that I had a fracture. I was going to have a lengthy lay-off. Greg had insisted that I carry on playing but I knew that now I was unable to play I would not be involved in anything to do with Salford RLFC. Greg appointed Steve Blakely as his captain and I recuperated at home with April and the boys. Salford went on to qualify for the Grand Finals to be played at Old Trafford but we did not receive an invitation and watched the game on the television. I felt upset by this as I had put my heart into Salford – we both had.

The transfer deal was sorted but a complication arose when Cardiff's transfer fee payment was late in coming through. That set off a game of cat-and-mouse with Salford saying the deal was off. Greg phoned me at home to tell me, perhaps thinking that I would really panic, but I did not show any emotion at all. I called their bluff by saying that I was happy to stay with them, but inside I had a sinking feeling as I felt that the deal had gone too far forward. I had possibly burnt my bridges with Salford. The fans had been loyal and supportive during my time at Salford but how would they react to a player who had publicly stated that he wanted to leave? I was left in no man's land. I turned up for training that evening putting out the vibes that I was happy to be staying. Inwardly, I was a mess. I was preparing to move my family to Wales and this had happened. Being happy was the furthest emotion from my mind.

Greg, I suspect, was in a panic. Richard Webster had already transferred to Bath so I was the joker in the pack. He set about his task of making sure that the deal was closed as soon as possible. Behind the scenes Peter Thomas again stepped in and sorted everything out. I was particularly grateful when he phoned April one day to reassure her that everything was in hand. It was a nice touch. He was undoubtedly the key man in a deal that was finally done in weeks rather than months.

As for Greg he telephoned to say that he had managed to get the deal back on track and had the cheek to add that I owed him a few pints. He felt that he had helped me gain a longer and more financially rewarding career.

9

BACK TO THE BLUE AND BLACKS

'Why have you come back?'

Those were almost the first words spoken to me as Cardiff staged a big press conference to welcome me back to Wales. They put on quite a show as I was one of four big signings that summer as the club added to a squad they hoped would push for top honours in both Wales and Europe with the Heineken Cup. Alongside me were three members of the Wales team from the previous season: Rob Howley, Justin Thomas and Leigh Davies. There were never half measures at the Arms Park!

So what about that $64,000 question?

Before I could answer, the local journalist had thrown in his own suggestion, that I had probably had enough of rugby league in the north of England. Nothing could have been further from the truth. I was quick to point out that rugby union had a much bigger profile and a much greater audience world wide than rugby league, which had only a pocket audience in the north of England and the southern hemisphere. With professionalism the union audience was only going to increase. It was something that I wanted to be a part of and realistically I thought that I would enjoy a much longer playing career as a union forward than as a league forward.

I was also quizzed as to whether Cardiff had been the only option. I admitted that there had been approaches from English clubs as well as Swansea. There had even been the possibility of staying in the Manchester area and playing for Sale. After long discussions April and I had decided that playing for an English club would not be an option as after my playing days were over we would want to move back to Wales. We did not want to keep shifting our children from school to school and felt strongly that a move at this time had to be the last. I therefore felt Cardiff was the only option.

Even as the questions piled in I could sense that I was well and truly back into the hotbed of rugby that exists only in South Wales. To be absolutely honest, it's good for the old ego to think that you're back in the limelight. Everyone likes a bit of a fuss and I knew that I was looking forward to playing again in Wales and particularly at the Arms Park. But as the press probed and probed the alarm bells could easily have started ringing. In the north of England I had enjoyed a bit of space. April and I could go out for a meal without being drawn into conversation by total strangers. If the odd person in Worsley recognised me it would be only to pass on good wishes or just to say 'Hello'. When Manchester United are on your doorstep the captain of the rugby league club is just another sportsman. In Wales it was very different.

I had forgotten in the six years I had been away just how intense the public gaze in Wales was and I hadn't realised that, if anything, the media's monitoring of your every move had also stepped up a gear. Years of failure by the Wales team and the apparent dismissal by critics outside Wales of the quality of the club scene had led to a lot of soul-searching and endless articles about how a proud rugby nation could get back on its feet. And the brunt of the responsibility seemed to lie with the players.

The first 18 months back in Wales were difficult. I would have to admit that at times the situation was unbearable. Step out anywhere and you could be drawn into a 20-minute chat by someone who wanted to give you his or her deep analysis of exactly where you or your team mates were going wrong. Every man and his dog was ready to offer advice. In the days after a loss people would look at you as if you were something they would not like to clean off their shoes. On one occasion, taking my children to school, the lollipop lady shouted across, 'Hey Dai, you boys were shit on Saturday.' On another memorable occasion when April was taking my two elder sons to school, after our heavy loss to England, the headmaster asked, 'And where is your husband today, Mrs Young? Ashamed to show his face?' Thomas and Lewis looked enquiringly on. The pressures at Cardiff were almost as great as those I felt when playing for Wales because there seems to be a universal hatred aimed at Cardiff as a club.

And then there was the press. Those questions at the first press conference were, I suppose, understandable and fairly harmless but as time went on I came to appreciate the power the newspapers and broadcasters in Wales had acquired in influencing the public. Matters would come to a head four years later when several writers hounded

Graham Henry and the coaching set-up in the national squad. In comparison, the atmosphere in 1996 was all sweetness and light though I couldn't help wondering what my three new team mates at Cardiff made of it all.

Howley, Thomas and Davies were internationals in their own right but it must have been a culture shock to find themselves in the Arms Park spotlight. Every move at the club is monitored and there is no shortage of people waiting to pounce when things go wrong. Rob is a class act at scrum-half who had already dipped his toes into the Arms Park water a couple of years earlier but had lasted only a few weeks before packing his bags and returning to Bridgend. There had been one or two stories flying around about him not getting on with the club's Aussie coach Alex Evans. Now, older, wiser and capped he was trying again with the no-nonsense coach safely back in Brisbane – or so he thought.

Justin and Leigh were prominent members of the new generation of backs who it was hoped would lead a rebirth of exciting 15-man rugby. Leigh, in particular, had made a big impression in his first internationals and there was every sign that Peter Thomas had done the right thing in bringing the two of them plus Rob Howley into the club squad. Both players were young and subsequently they were both to experience the first season syndrome where they received nothing but unrelenting criticism and pressure from the media, who seemed to expect more because they were wearing the blue and black jersey. The result was that both players lost confidence and their form suffered.

Rob, the oldest of the three at nearly 26, had waited quite a long time to break into the national side but had finally been given the chance to show that he was a world class scrum-half. All of them carried that air of excitement about being involved at the big city club.

With Alex Evans back in Australia the coaching team at the Arms Park was headed by Terry Holmes. I found this very reassuring because he was someone that I had the greatest respect for as a player and as a man and in the next couple of years he didn't disappoint me as a coach either. The bullets that fly in the direction of the Arms Park from outside usually carry the message that the club doesn't develop its own talent and that it is always looking for the quick fix by bringing in star players and big-name coaches for big bucks.

Terry Holmes was the living proof that such comments were nothing more than blind prejudice. Here was a man who had been born and bred in the city, played for the youth team, and made his debut for the first team when he was barely 18 years old. He went on to captain the club and Wales before going north to play for Bradford Northern. It was typical of his heroic approach to the game that he had taken on the mighty task of coaching Cardiff without the traditional grounding of time spent with a junior club as he learnt his trade.

Terry had obviously benefited from his two years as Alex Evans' assistant but once he was in charge he was the same forthright character he had always been. It couldn't have been easy taking over from Evans, who had arrived from Australia almost like a knight on a white charger, regenerating the club after the humiliation of near-relegation (which they had escaped on a technicality) to pick up league and cup titles in a three-year period. He had departed midway through the previous season but Terry had taken over and the team had reached the first European Cup final and finished second in the league, only being pipped for top spot on try-count. Even when I arrived six months later you could sense that Evans had left a shadow over the club that any successor would find hard to shake off. But Terry was a straight talker who didn't pull any punches and, I have to admit, I was surprised by how much he had embraced all aspects of professionalism. He was a man of action who had learnt how to handle the tools of the trade such as video analysis and flip charts and all the other paraphernalia of modern sport. More than anything he always stuck up for the players. He was not afraid to tell you when you were out of order but, first and foremost, Terry Holmes was a player's man.

The great tragedy was that Terry was never allowed to finish the job he started. In the course of the next two years, he suffered demotion to number two on the return of Alex Evans. This turned out to be a short-lived and ill-conceived revisiting of former glories. Reinstated as number one after Alex's departure for a second time he then felt he had to resign for good after an admittedly disastrous cup defeat by Llanelli.

There was no sign of the changes to come when I touched base with the Cardiff squad. My first training session was at the Cardiff High School for Boys ground in Whitchurch and I was welcomed with open arms by Terry's right-hand man, Charlie Faulkner. Terry Homes may have been Cardiff to the core and Charlie may have been a proud man of Gwent but it was as if they were hewn from the same rock. They were men from working-class backgrounds who, as Terry once said, had received their education in the university of life. 'Cardiff Rugby Club was my university,' was his proud boast.

Where Terry had been the bravest and strongest of scrum-halves, Charlie had been the supreme scrummager who won his first cap when he was 34 and was still playing international rugby four years later. Like Terry, Charlie had learnt his coaching techniques by practice rather than theory, in his case with a spell at Newport. He was the ideal man to sort out my set-piece play after six years away from rugby union.

Charlie Faulkner knew forward play inside out. He had helped to establish a formidable pack at Cardiff. One of his prides was a prop called Lyndon Mustoe. He had cut his teeth at the Pontypool club and this was a source of great delight for Charlie, himself one-third of the legendary Pontypool front row – or, as they were less affectionately known, the 'Viet-Gwent'. Under the master's tutelage, Mustoe had won his first cap and Cardiff could already boast an all-international front row before I arrived. The loose-head prop was Andrew Lewis, a mobile young player who had already shown signs of being one of the best all-round props produced in recent years.

Completing the trio was Jonathan Humphreys and it was ironic that he was one of the first to greet me at the training session. Six years before I had shared a pint with Humph and his big mate Paul John in the Cardiff clubhouse on that fateful evening when I had announced that I was going north. Then he was a young forward more than a trifle bemused by the shenanigans going on around him. I had sought solace in his company after Alan Phillips had questioned my need to turn professional on purely financial grounds. Now, in 1996, he was as worldly-wise as the next man, a battle-hardened hooker who was captain of Wales. Times had certainly changed!

As I was to find out at first hand over the next five years Jonathan Humphreys was the most competitive and committed hooker I had ever played with. He would sometimes put his head where others would not put their feet and if there was one criticism of him it would be that when he became captain of Wales he took on too much himself in every game. Years later when I found myself in the same situation I understood better why captaincy had affected him that way. Being a whole-hearted player, he was absolutely desperate to lead a successful side from the front. He brought a new meaning to that over-used phrase, 'putting your body on the line' but that's exactly what he did. Along the way he picked up an unfair reputation for killing the ball at rucks. Some of the barracking from opposition supporters became ridiculous. I began to think that some of the first words the fans at Stradey Park and Sardis Road shouted when they were toddlers must have been 'Offside Humphreys'! But I know one thing for sure, when the going gets tough I would have Humph at my side every time.

So there they were: an all-international front row of Lewis, Humphreys and Mustoe, backed up by one of the most promising young props in Wales – Phil Booth; and at my first training session Charlie Faulkner had a special job for them – to give Dai the scrummaging practice he desperately needed. I knew from day one that Charlie was going to be my shadow but that was no problem because I had come across him during my first stint in union and now he wanted to work with me night and day. So Lyndon, Alp, Boothy and Humph were conscripted to join me for extra sessions on the scrummaging machine to knock me back into shape. To their great credit they did just that without any mutterings and moans – and there was a lot to do.

The new laws in union meant that a prop's shoulders had to stay above waist height and his back had to be straight. Frankly, this was a device that favoured every loose-head in the business. The number one shirt had been the toughest position in the scrum but now the onus had shifted to number three. Charlie knew that a lot of work was needed on my feet positions and body alignment. So we got to work and, with everyone's help and patience, as the weeks went by David Young became a rugby union prop again.

In some respects it was a race against time because within four weeks Cardiff were due to start their Heineken Cup campaign. The first match was away, at Wasps, and since the club had reached the European final the year before everyone was talking about going one step further and becoming Champions of Europe. The last thing I wanted was to be thrown in at the deep end but with my preparations going well Terry Holmes felt I should make my union comeback in a club match at the Arms Park. There was a bit of extra pressure on me because we had lost the first three league games, which was almost unheard of, and then scraped a one-point win at Treorchy. Fortunately the team had struck a bit of form after that with a couple of wins so the visit of Bridgend seemed the right time to re-introduce me to competitive rugby union.

I watched from the replacements' bench for the first hour of the match, increasingly anxious to be called on. As always when playing Bridgend, the game was pretty close and as always there were one or two things going on that didn't impress me at all. A few of their pack seemed to be taking pot shots at our giant lock Derwyn Jones as he came down from the lineouts. This had riled me more than a little and by the time I was eventually called on as a replacement with a quarter-of-an-hour left I was, you might say, fairly hyped up. We immediately had three or four scrums and I felt amazingly comfortable thanks to Charlie. When we had our first lineout Derwyn caught the ball with both hands but on his way down the Bridgend hooker Ian Greenslade (or Compo), a former Cardiff player who could always be counted on to be in the middle of things, swung a punch. So I retaliated.

The referee had seen what had happened and I was summoned for a lecture and perhaps worse. Suddenly I could see the next day's headlines, 'Dai sent off in disgrace!' Both teams had already been warned that the next incident by either side would lead to someone getting a red card so the situation wasn't at all promising. Luckily our captain for the day was Jonathan Davies and he raced over to us shouting 'First offence, ref, first offence . . . and Dai wasn't on the field when you gave the warning!' Looking back on it I'm not sure whether the official, Huw Lewis, was correct in accepting Jiffy's instant interpretation but to my great relief he gave me the benefit of the doubt, only waved a yellow card at me, and I stayed on. Greenslade went very quiet and we won the game.

Naturally I was pleased with my brief contribution to a good team performance and the press spotlight turned not only on me but also on Charlie. He came up with some purlers at the post-match interviews. Wales had played France in a friendly match on the Wednesday before and Charlie wasn't at all impressed with the way the pack had struggled.

'We need to beef up the pack,' he said. 'We lost against France because there was no physical presence – we've got pace but no beef but now we have ready-made beef from up north.'

Beef, beef, beef! Charlie went on, 'David Young has presence. He was in trouble with the referee as soon as he came on only because he would not take any messing. Olivier Merle would not have had so much to say for France if Dai had been around. His return is the best news Welsh rugby has had for a while.'

Obviously comments like that from someone I respected were a huge ego-boost but I still felt it was far too soon to jump to any conclusions about a glorious return to international rugby union. In time-honoured fashion my comments to the press after the Bridgend match were that I would take one match at a time and just enjoy it. Deep down, though, I knew that the spotlight on me would not go away. I had already been drafted into the Wales squad for the internationals against Australia, USA and South Africa in a couple of months' time and the Welsh Rugby Union had honoured Terry Cobner's promise to employ me as a development officer. You couldn't blame them for wanting something in return.

I had another run-out as a replacement in a club match against Harlequins. This was not the high-powered encounter you would normally expect between the two clubs but an ill-fated competition called the Anglo-Welsh League. The matches were played mid-week but the Quins and others soon gave notice of their intentions by fielding second-string sides. The weekend fixtures in their domestic league were far more important to them and by November the cross-border contests had petered out. The only meaningful matches with the pride of English club rugby would be in the Heineken Cup and, as luck would have it, Cardiff's first tie had thrown up an away match with Wasps in London.

This was the perfect platform to make my first full appearance. It was sure to be a tough game with a lot at stake. We couldn't afford to lose what we hoped would be the first step on the long road to European glory. As expected, the Wasps fielded some of the big names in English rugby, including Sheasby, Dallaglio and Will Green, but there was somebody very familiar to me at loose-head – Mike Griffiths. It could only happen to me. Here I was back trying to prove that I was in tip-top form as a scrummager as well as a ball-carrier and tackler and packing down directly opposite me was my biggest mate!

Griff seemed to find the whole situation immensely funny but I knew that he couldn't afford to give me an inch. He was new to Wasps himself having left Cardiff a few months before I arrived. He had been joking during the summer that he had only departed so that there would be a gap for me to fill and he was smoothing my path for me to make a name for myself. Now, in the intensity of a European match, he could ruin everything. I was surprisingly nervous before the match and, once it had started, Griff and I locked horns in the scrums. Whenever we had a lineout he had a big grin on his face but I knew he was putting everything into the game. It was obvious that as a former British Lion himself and a renowned tight-forward, the rest of the Wasps pack looked up to him and he wasn't going to disappoint them. But I did well and by the end of the game the experience had been a great confidence-builder. To complete a happy day we sneaked a win thanks to a Jonathan Davies dropped goal in the dying seconds. It was just as well Jiffy delivered the goods in a situation that was made for him because for most of the previous 80 minutes he had had a shocker. But that was typical Jiffy, always capable of turning a result on its head with a moment of individual brilliance.

Whatever the future held with Wales, I now felt part and parcel of the Cardiff squad. It was a particularly strong pack. As well as the front row permutations, it was deadly effective in winning lineout ball. Wherever he went, Derwyn Jones received a lot of stick. Perhaps it was because of his size, because at six feet ten inches tall he stood out wherever he went. Like Jonathan Humphreys and one or two others, Derwyn had been a major beneficiary of the coaching of Alex Evans. He had arrived at the Arms Park four years before for a holiday match and the club had immediately recognised his potential. The 1990s were not a golden era for Welsh lineout play but Evans made him superbly effective. Within 18 months he was playing for Wales. He was an obvious target for opposition skulduggery – Ian Greenslade was not the first guy to try illegally to reduce his effectiveness – but through it all Derwyn was remarkably committed.

The barracking he received from the terraces would have been enough to demoralise lesser players but Derwyn never threw in the towel and he was never bitter. In my book, as a player he was hugely underestimated. He 'bossed' the lineouts in every match he played and this wasn't achieved by accident or simply because of his height. What the fans didn't see was the endless hours he spent studying videos of his opponents. Alex Evans had showed him the Promised Land and Derwyn was determined to enjoy as much of it as he could. He was a good scrummager and I always wanted him packing down behind me in the right-hand lock position. Three years after I arrived, Derwyn left the club to play in France and shortly after that he gave up playing. I was sorry to see him go.

Never far away from Derwyn Jones in every lineout was Hemi Taylor. Whoever said that the Cardiff pack had a soft underbelly had never encountered Hemi. Born and brought up in New Zealand he was the hard edge of the pack. In my first year he was club captain and he certainly led from the front. As a ball carrier, particularly from the back of a scrum, he was outstanding with his charges always certain to cause the home crowd to erupt. What he received little credit for was his ability to off-load the ball at the right time and the people who really benefited from that were his supporting players.

Hemi was always in the middle of everything and his defence was faultless but it would be foolish to pretend that he endeared himself to many crowds away from the Arms Park. If it wasn't Jonathan Humphreys getting the bird for allegedly killing the ball, or Derwyn Jones hounded for guaranteeing our ball in every lineout, it was Hemi Taylor copping it for his abrasive play and all-consuming tackles. Perhaps they missed the point, we were simply a very good pack of forwards.

It would be foolish to pretend, though, that the team was the finished article. My first season coincided with a period of change, particularly in the backs. Mike Rayer, a blue and black icon, had left after 12 seasons with the club at full-back and both half-backs, Andy Moore and Adrian Davies, had transferred to Richmond. None of these departures had been well received by the membership at large as everyone was impatient for further success and they saw these departing players as part of that success. But the future rested literally in the hands of the new signings, Howley, Davies and Thomas, under the guidance of Jonathan Davies, Nigel Walker and the previous club captain, Mike Hall. Jonathan was perhaps considered to be past his best but still at his age was world class. I consider Jiffy to be the most talented all round rugby player I have ever played with. In Mike Hall we had one of the most committed, hard-tackling and elusive runners ever to play for Cardiff, and who had great game-awareness. Mike never knew when he was beaten. Nigel Walker was very much underrated; his speed was phenomenal and his defensive work was always of the highest order.

The Wasps victory had set us up well for the remainder of the pool matches in the Heineken Cup and further wins over Munster and Milan qualified us for a home quarter-final against Bath. That attracted a full house to the Arms Park and, for the first time in my experience, there was some boisterous singing and chanting as we won the game 22–19. That, unfortunately, was almost the end of our European campaign as we lost the semi-final in Brive.

It was indicative of the ingrained habit of seeking instant remedies that, with barely a month of the season left, and with the team already comfortably qualified for the semi-final of the Swalec Cup, Alex Evans was brought back from Australia to be director of rugby. One or two of the senior players welcomed this Second Coming as if all Cardiff's problems, whatever they were, would be swept away overnight; others, I sensed, were more sceptical. For my part, I reserved judgement for the time being. I had heard so much about Alex Evans but over the 13 months he was with the club – that's how long his second term lasted – I was not impressed. He obviously knew the technical side of the game inside out. He was very capable of coaching any player in any position and any unit in the forwards or backs, but it was equally apparent that he did not want to be there. It soon became the norm for him to arrive for a training session five minutes before it was due to start and leave immediately after it had finished. After a while, all his training sessions became identical, and it seemed obvious that he had not spent time preparing for the sessions – not the behaviour of a dedicated director of rugby.

I understand one of his relatives was ill so he was naturally concerned for their welfare, and also I don't think that his personal health was A1. His job, in addition, was very different from when he had first arrived. Then he had been the archetypal track-suited coach who got to grips with everything on the training field. Now he was expected to take on all the other duties, many of them office-bound, of a director of rugby. It was also a time when the club's administration was in some turmoil and several meetings were held to consider the establishment of a limited company run by a board of businessmen – admittedly enthusiastic rugby-men – rather than a committee of elected volunteers. Evans was nominated to be on the board of directors and I very much doubt whether he really wanted to be part of that.

The team did him proud with an exciting win over Swansea in the Swalec Cup final shortly after he arrived but the next season, his first full one back in charge, was undistinguished. We went out of both the European and Welsh Cups in the quarter-finals and finished second in the league. Forty-eight hours after our final fixture Alex Evans flew home to Australia and during the summer that followed his contract was terminated by mutual agreement. He never returned.

I have been in the proximity of Alex on several occasions since his departure, the latest being in Australia with the Lions of 2001. I think that Alex must be under the impression that I had something to do with his departure as he goes out of his way to avoid conversation with me, but saying that he never spoke to me during his time at Cardiff either. To put the record straight I never did have any input into the reasons for his departure.

10

BOWRING'S WALES

It wasn't only Charlie Faulkner who thought I should be playing for Wales from the moment I returned to Cardiff. I found myself straight back in the national squad that was preparing for the pre-Christmas internationals against Australia, USA and South Africa. It would be foolish to deny that this wasn't a boost to my confidence and at the same time confirmation that I had done the right thing in signing a union contract. The Welsh Rugby Union, in the shape of Terry Cobner, had been instrumental in working with Cardiff's chairman Peter Thomas to dot the i's and cross the t's on the finer points. Once I was back in South Wales, I began the job as a development officer that had been floated in the air over six years before. This time it was a reality and I had no qualms whatsoever about my responsibilities. They involved public relations work, presentations and what I thoroughly enjoyed about this was that it brought me into contact with the grass roots of the game.

Kevin Bowring, with the help of Cobner, was in the middle of establishing a 'Club Wales' mentality whereby 20 players, in the first instance, would combine their playing careers with a development officer's role. In other words, we had dual contracts. We were required to train with the Wales squad on three mornings every week, and return to our clubs for yet more training in the afternoons. Once the initial excitement of being part of the international scene had died down and I had settled into a regular routine I became aware that the situation was potentially very stressful.

There were several issues to consider, not least the fact that we were working with two different fitness coaches, both good in their own right but both wanting to do what they considered the best for their respective masters; masters who set them different objectives and goals.

Dave Clark, a South African who had recently been appointed as fitness coach for Wales, wanted to, in his words, 'increase the muscular strength and power of the players'. He was very professional, organised and totally committed to raising us to a new level of fitness. As the international season continues over a full year Dave trained us to peak for each international which meant training through club fixtures. His opinion was that the level of fitness required for an international was higher than that for a club game and the only way to achieve that higher level was sometimes to play a club game with some fatigue hangover from his training. Although this was explained to and agreed by all clubs prior to the commencement of the season, in reality it was never going to work. Clubs have their own priorities and while they were always 100 per cent behind the Welsh cause they had to protect their jobs as they would be judged on club results and not international ones. There was no escaping the fact that all the players in Club Wales were stuck in the middle, serving two masters with two different agendas, so at the end of the day it would only be the players that would suffer.

The other issue, of course, was that a rugby team was judged by its results and we all wanted to do well so there were few complaints if Cardiff and Wales kept winning. That, unfortunately, was not the case with Wales. As I have said, the return of so many former union internationals from the league code had sparked off a wave of anticipation. Almost without exception all of us who had made the trek back to the homeland had been put straight into the national squad. Alongside me that autumn were Scott Gibbs, Allan Bateman and Jonathan Davies and, shortly after Christmas, Scott Quinnell was recruited as well. Whatever pressure we felt was probably nothing compared to the weight of responsibility on the shoulders of the national coach, Kevin Bowring, who was ultimately responsible for pulling us all together as a team.

Bowring was now in his second season in charge and there had been encouraging signs in his first season when Wales had run England close at Twickenham and, though losing unluckily to Scotland and heavily to Ireland, had finished with an uplifting win over France. He had also shown the courage of his convictions by selecting young midfield backs and had given Rob Howley an overdue debut at the top level. The team had since toured Australia and lost heavily. I sensed when I first met Rob Howley, Leigh Davies and Justin Thomas (even though Justin himself has not been on the tour) that the Wallaby experience had sown the seeds of self-doubt in their minds. There seemed to be a danger of putting southern hemisphere teams on a pedestal. On the other hand, I was impressed by their motivation to turn things around. But whether or not they could was partly dependent on the quality of Bowring's coaching.

At the time I arrived he was very upbeat, positive and brimming over with enthusiasm for his task. He was not the first coach to proclaim that his philosophy was for his team to play 'good rugby' but with Kevin you really believed it. The results had not gone his way but he now had an improving management structure in place to support him. Kevin had himself worked his way through the representative coaching ranks with Wales under-21 and Wales A and there was every indication that he would be reasonably successful at the top of the pyramid. He had a team of advisers that included a scrum coach and a back-coach and he went around all the clubs to share his ideas. I liked him because he was obviously a sincere man who would do everything in his power to help a player. That was certainly true in my case. I may have been a one-time Lions' test prop and I may have been doing well again with Cardiff in rugby union, but in international terms I was being fast-tracked back onto the big stage.

I was earmarked to wear the Wales jersey again after what was a nearly seven-year gap on 1 December 1996 when Australia came to the National Stadium. By then I would have played five full club games and had a couple of appearances as a replacement. This was hardly ideal preparation and Kevin was anxious to supplement the help I was getting from Charlie Faulkner at the club. He worked with me a lot on a one-to-one basis, even going so far as to monitor my running-lines between breakdowns. His own scrummaging coach, John Moore, was also at hand and by the time the big day came I could have no complaints about the preparation and back-up I had received from all concerned. If I had any anxiety, it was that I would be the first league player to reappear as an international union forward – Scott Quinnell would follow me a couple of matches later. I felt sure that I would attract a lot of attention but, thankfully, the situation changed four days before the game.

Kevin Bowring had chosen Arwel Thomas at fly-half as he had for most of his games since becoming coach, but on the Monday before the Australian test Arwel dropped out. At first it was assumed that Neil Jenkins would fill the gap but, instead, Jonathan Davies was recalled to the number ten shirt for his country. Suddenly, the media spotlight left me! Here was the marketing men's dream to end all dreams come true. Jonathan was in a different category from the rest of us when the fans and the media speculated as to what had happened to Welsh rugby when we had all gone north. Never ones to bog ourselves down with a dose of cold realism, Welsh fans would happily fantasise about the mythical fly-half factory that had regularly produced little men of magic to win rugby matches for us. And when Jonathan had gone to league, so the delusion continued, the production line dried up. Now he was back . . . glory awaited us.

It could only happen in Wales and within 72 hours the WRU had sold another 10,000–15,000 tickets for a match that had looked likely to be played in a half-empty stadium. The original crowd estimate accurately reflected what the fans thought of our chances of winning as much as it did the counter-attractions and expense of Christmas shopping. On the day, 45,000 turned up, by no means a capacity crowd, but Jonathan didn't disappoint them, with a first-minute penalty goal and four more successful kicks in the match. We lost 19–28 but it was a fairly encouraging result for all concerned. Away from the spotlight I was able to find my feet, coping pretty well with the challenge of my opposite number, Dan Crowley, in the scrums and generally contributing some useful things around the field. It had been a big day for me, with April and my family attending. It had also been quite emotional as I had thought I would never again run out onto the National Stadium for Wales. Afterwards, I had a pint with Crowley, a good prop in his own right, and he was genuinely interested in how I had found the transition back from league to union. As I looked around the after-match reception it was obvious that one thing had certainly not changed in my years away – the room was still full of committee-men and their wives enjoying the fruits of professional rugby. Unfortunately, Kevin Bowring's shelf-life as national coach proved to be less enduring.

We picked up a couple of good results in the next year, including a high-scoring win at Murrayfield when the bounce of the ball was definitely with us. That sent everybody into cartwheels as they proclaimed the dawn of a new era. It ended abruptly with three defeats in a row. Worse was to follow in 1997–98 when the home matches were being played at Wembley while the Millennium Stadium was under construction. We were not expected to beat the All Blacks and didn't disappoint the forecasters. Even so, we thought we would do better than 0–29 down at half-time on the way to a 40-points' stuffing. The pressure really was on Kevin now. An even greater indignity was heaped on us at Twickenham as we slumped to a 60-point hammering. After a good start with a couple of Allan Bateman tries, we were ripped apart in the closing stages and the mood in the camp after that bordered on despair. It was definitely a time to stay indoors in the days that followed.

On the Monday Kevin held a debriefing session at Cardiff and encouraged everyone to speak openly about the defeat. Some players said that they felt unable to venture outside their houses, others said that they felt they had let everyone down. When Kevin asked me I replied truthfully that I hoped he would pick someone else for the next game. I could take the criticism and cope with the disappointment of losing the game, but no one understands how much your family feel your hurt and I did not want to put them through that again. This defeat was particularly dreadful because individually we felt that we were better than England.

With an international every fortnight there was barely time to recover, but recover we had to. We gained a win over Scotland after we had been outplayed for large chunks of the match. There seemed some light at the end of the tunnel when we had a good win in Dublin – forgetting, perhaps, that Ireland were themselves heading for a whitewash in the championship. Although we left it late, on our scrum deep in Irish territory Stuart Davies picked up and ran blind and with the Irish flanker accidentally tripping over Colin's foot – good one Colin – leaving space for Stuart to run, feeding Neil Jenkins who ran in unopposed. However, a final horror awaited us on our third visit to Wembley.

This time it was France who ran us ragged, to the tune of 51 points. It's easy to say that it was one of those days when the French played as only they can, but in our heart of hearts we knew that the national team had reached a crossroads. We had let Kevin Bowring down but when the recriminations started, as they immediately did, it was he who paid the ultimate price. It is common knowledge that we don't back our Welsh coaches when things go wrong and there was no point in any of us pretending that Kevin Bowring could survive this situation. Yet to his great credit he produced a blueprint for the future. It included a streamlined domestic season built around an Anglo-Welsh league, a plan for four regional teams in the Heineken Cup that would give the top players high-class competition with a reasonable chance of success, and a widening of the centralised contracts scheme for the international squad. He also wanted to strengthen his own back-room staff with specialist coaches for skills and positions.

I realised that Kevin's position based on results that included only four wins in twelve Five Nations' matches had become untenable, but I was sorry to see him go. His views on the way forward for Welsh rugby were correct. When the knives were out, the critics conveniently forgot that Kevin Bowring had worked hard to develop players like Colin Charvis. All sorts of nonsense was spouted forth, including the one about him being a schoolteacher and therefore ill suited to the management of players. No one had said that when he was in charge of the under-21 and A team and no one said it about his successor when Graham Henry was appointed.

I am amazed that Kevin's qualities as a coach have not been more fully used in the years since his departure. He now coaches the aspiring players of UWIC, a great rugby nursery in Cardiff University, but he is something of a forgotten man. Typically, he has not forgotten those of us he guided on to greater things. Two years after he was sacked, he wrote a personal letter to me after my appointment as captain of Wales. He made no effort to hide the fact that his tenure in charge had ended with the French humiliation, but he could also see the positives in every situation.

He wrote: 'Gain confidence from the fact that your leadership qualities are obvious, have been recognised and that you have the respect of the players and management. Those qualities were certainly evident when you returned to the game from rugby league. I remember saying to you a few years ago that we had to rebuild our scrum and asked for your help. Two years ago we may have been hammered by France at Wembley, but we won the scrummage battle and I felt that we had started the rebuilding process. I am pleased that you have continued with it over the past couple of seasons.'

His letter ended: 'Please pass on good luck wishes to all the players and management and wish them every success.'

That generosity of spirit was so typical of Kevin Bowring. I will be forever indebted to him for his major part in my reintegration into international rugby union.

11

THE LURE OF THE LIONS

I doubt whether any sportsman or sportswoman could ever get near to achieving anything in their chosen sport without ambition and motivation to go with whatever ability they might have. That is certainly true in my case and especially so when I won selection for the British and Irish Lions of 2001. In terms of motivation, the story might start as long ago as my first Lions' tour, at the age of 21 in 1989. That, after all, was when I tasted the thrill of everything that goes with such a tour, not least being in a winning test side. I might also throw in the pot the memories of the aggro that came my way from the Aussie press and some of their officials. It was quite an attraction to think that I might return to Sydney, Brisbane and Melbourne and do it all over again!

In all honesty, though, the road to the 2001 tour really started in 1997 when I went to South Africa full of hope after successfully re-establishing myself as a union prop only to be left kicking my heels in frustration because of what I considered a lack of opportunities. The gloss of being a Lion for a second time gradually wore off as I realised that the forwards' coach, Jim Telfer, was never going to give me a chance to prove my test match credentials. What happened on that tour proved the greatest incentive possible to try to become a Lion again, even when I was struck down by a series of potentially demoralising injuries.

It need not have been that way. The build-up to South Africa in 1997 had been full of positives from my point of view. First of all there was the great carrot of being the first prop to return from rugby league to be even considered for selection for the British team. There was only nine months in which to do this but I always thought that I was in with a chance. Few top-quality tight-heads existed in the British Isles and I felt I had performed creditably in my first two internationals before Christmas against the Wallabies and Springboks. Wales had also played a fairly low-key warm-up game against the USA Eagles and by the time the Five Nations matches were under way in mid-January I had already been named in the provisional list of 65 players for the Lions.

That was a huge pick-me-up and when we met in Birmingham I was immediately struck by the professionalism surrounding the whole operation. Even at that relatively early stage the management were very thorough in their preparation. We were given an outline on how the players' contracts would work and we were taken through the timetable for selection and for the lucky ones four months later the arrangements for pre-tour training. No stone was left unturned to the extent that every one of the 65 of us on the long list were measured up by Adidas for our training and playing kit and by Next for our formal wear. All of this made us want even more to be part of the final 35 names to be announced in April!

When that announcement came I expected it to be via the television set at home. I had found it difficult in the few days beforehand to second-guess my realistic chances of selection. The Five Nations matches had been a mixed bag because although I had played in all four games for Wales the results had deteriorated during the championship. We had played fairly well to win an exciting match at Murrayfield and that again had everyone doing cartwheels in Wales. After that we had come down to earth with a bang. We scored a try from the kick-off in our next match against Ireland at Cardiff and then proceeded to lose a game that was there for the taking. We played much better in Paris but still lost. The final indignity was that we were well beaten by England in the last-ever game at the National Stadium in Cardiff before it was demolished.

It was generally accepted that England would provide the majority of the Lions' party and as things turned out they numbered 18 of the original 35, including a complete pack. I was not surprised that Jason Leonard was in pole-position for tight-head. After all, he was a good player in a Triple Crown-winning side, but would I be there with him vying for the test match position?

It was a letter that provided the answer when an hour before the press conference was shown live on television the postman brought the best news possible. The letter was dated 1 April but this was deadly serious and I have to admit the sense of satisfaction of having again reached the top of the union game was tremendous. My scrummaging had received the seal of approval and for that I will be eternally grateful to Charlie Faulkner in particular. My general game was also up to scratch and for that I also had to thank Kevin Bowring and Terry Holmes, the Cardiff coach.

Not for the first time, Kevin was among the first to congratulate me and, as always, offered sensible advice. 'Go with an open mind,' he wrote, 'and with a willingness to learn and with the confidence to meet the challenge. When you return it will be as a better player and hopefully motivated to help Wales continue their improvement.'

I had no reason to disagree with his sentiments and looked forward to becoming a Lion again with a hunger that surprised even myself. We seemed to have a strong touring party, managed by Fran Cotton, coached by Ian McGeechan for the third time, led by Martin Johnson, and with strength and depth in every position. A particular interest for me, naturally, was the composition of the front row. Tom Smith had seemed to come from nowhere to claim one of the loose-head berths but the test spot according to all the pundits was earmarked for Graham Rowntree. There was also a possibility of Jason reverting to loose-head with me on the tight-head. There were three hookers with Keith Wood probably the top-man and then there were two other tight-heads apart from myself. All three of us knew our way around.

As expected Jason Leonard had deservedly won selection for his second Lions' tour. Jason is a great guy for whom I have the utmost respect. I knew him to be an honest bloke who was a role model for any young player. He had played over 40 times for England before he moved across from loose-head to establish himself as a tight-head. Not surprisingly, when the 1997 tour finally got under way we spent a lot of time together and, despite the rivalry for the test shirt, always got on well.

The original selection as the third tight-head was Ireland's Peter Clohessy and this was a bit of a surprise. Although he was an established international player in his own right he had spent the winter in Australia preparing to play in the Super 12s with Queensland and had not featured in the pre-tour selections. He had obviously been monitored by the selectors and was called back to become a Lion. However, when he turned up at our first get-together in Dalmahoy it was discovered that he had a back problem. Every one of us felt for Peter, as he was withdrawn from the squad. To pull out at that stage with everyone together for the first time and preparing for the great adventure ahead must be the worst possible situation to be in. Little did I know that four years later the gods would conspire to put me on the brink of the same misfortune.

With Clohessy out of the reckoning, his fellow Irishman, Paul

Wallace, was drafted in at the eleventh hour. We knew him to be one of the younger generation of props. With a couple of seasons in the Ireland team already under his belt, he wouldn't weaken the squad in any way. I have to admit, I privately thought it would be a straight fight between Jason and myself for the test spot. I couldn't have been more wrong. Paul Wallace was to have an outstanding tour – and a further obstacle to my prospects was what proved to be an insurmountable problem with Jim Telfer.

Telfer has deservedly gained a big reputation in world rugby for his achievements as a Lion in his playing days. He was an automatic first choice on two tours in the 1960s and in 1983 had coached the Lions in New Zealand. With Scotland he was famed for an ability to produce the best performances imaginable from what were often limited resources. He seemed the perfect partner to Ian McGeechan, with specific responsibilities for the Lions' forwards. Knowing him to be particularly keen on a solid platform in the scrum, I thought that I would at least have a fair crack of the whip so that I could prove myself. I was sadly mistaken.

I knew that with three tight-heads in the squad and only 13 fixtures on the itinerary regular matches could not be taken for granted. On the other hand there was a good run-in to the first Test with eight games so I thought that, injuries permitting, I would start in three of them. It didn't quite work out that way.

Jason was picked for the first game at Port Elizabeth, with the added honour of the captaincy, and no one begrudged him that. Paul Wallace was on the bench. I was pleased to start the next game against Border, with Graham Rowntree at loose-head and Mark Regan at hooker. We went well but unfortunately the ground was very heavy and it was difficult to dominate our opponents in the set pieces. To make things worse we had a couple of downpours during the game and the pitch was more or less waterlogged. We only scraped a win by four points having missed several kicks at goal, but in the circumstances I had no reason to think that the team put out that night were in any way 'dirt-trackers'.

The alarm bells were still not ringing when I didn't feature at all in the next match, the first big Saturday game of the tour against Western Province at Newlands. Seven of the England pack were named in the starting line-up for that one, plus the Welsh hooker Barry Williams. But what really cheesed me off were the selections for the next two games at Witbank and Pretoria. Paul Wallace got the nod for one of them and Jason for the other. I was called on as a replacement both times, but only for five minutes at the end of each game. It was time for a heart-to-heart talk with the coach.

Ian McGeechan is a good listener and he understood my concerns. I admitted that no one was surprised that the English front five had started the tour as firm favourites to challenge for test places to take on the Springboks. All five of them had played against Northern Transvaal and we had lost. The front row had not dominated as had been expected. Telfer was on the warpath about the difficulties we had encountered in the scrum. If the scrum was creaking – and it certainly was against the Blue Bulls – then I felt that it was now my turn to have a high-profile game. Geech reassured me that I was not forgotten and that I should stick with it.

All I could do was take him at his word. The next match was against Gauteng Lions under the Ellis Park floodlights. This time Wallace won the starting berth but Geech and Telfer told me that we would have a half each – I would be called on at the interval. That seemed fair enough, if I wasn't in the starting line-up then I would settle for that. Half-time came and went and there was no sign of me being called on. As the clock ticked by in the second half I was becoming more and more frustrated. Finally, with less than a minute to go, one of the coaching staff, Andy Keast, who was down on the touchline shouted across, 'Dai, you're going on.'

My reply was short and sweet, 'You're joking!'

Andy replied, 'No I am not. Jim said get stripped off and on you go.'

I told Andy, 'Tell Jim to get fucked.'

I refused to take my track-suit off and seconds later the referee blew for full-time. Afterwards in the changing-room, Telfer came up to me and said, 'If I tell you to go on, you go on.'

I replied, 'You told me I was going on at half-time. By the time I had taken my track-suit off the game would have been finished. Show me some respect and I will give you the respect you deserve. Don't try to make a fool of me.'

I would be the first to admit that this was not a healthy state of affairs. We were on the first professional Lions' tour and matters should not have come to this. Respect between a player and a coach has to be mutual. Telfer's reputation in the sport is well deserved because he believes in doing the basics well and no one can question his commitment, thoroughness and enthusiasm. What he achieved in South Africa in 1997 will go down in the record books and it speaks for itself. But he definitely had a downer on me.

I wondered whether it was simply a case of a die-hard Scot, born and brought up in the true-blue amateurism north of the Border, having an ingrained disapproval of a forward who had played rugby league. Somehow that didn't stack up because there were five ex-league players in the original tour party, though Scott Quinnell was the only other forward. Perhaps it was something as ridiculous as an episode at the pre-tour camp in Weybridge when a player kicked the ball which hit his head from behind, knocking his glasses off and when he turned around he spotted me buckled up laughing. (I could not help myself!) Frankly I don't know what the root cause of the problem was but it never went away. I suspect that Telfer sees himself as a disciplinarian who likes to, for want of a better word, 'bully' people with no questions asked. I remember one occasion at training when Telfer wanted the forwards to ruck more vigorously using their boots and studs. In order for them to practise this he wanted me to lie on the ball on the ground so that they could run over me. You can guess what I told him.

Although I did support him 100 per cent both on and off the pitch, I also found a lot of his sayings and expressions humorous, especially when he told me that he wanted me to run as fast as I could, then accelerate. Another classic was he wanted me to be as sharp as a knife and as tight as a drum. Comments such as these always brought a smile to my face. Unfortunately it became a training ground joke amongst the players that I was always the fall guy for Telfer and that it seemed I could never do anything right. It has been mentioned by several players who were on the 1997 tour.

The longer the tour went on the more I felt as if I was being marginalised at training. Given Telfer's fondness for work on the scrum machine, I thought I would have played a bigger part in his plans. In the latter stages of the tour I more often than not was told to pack down on the flank. Before his own unfortunate injury that brought his tour to a premature end, Rob Howley, who was in the best position to know at scrum-half, had told me that I had the best score of any of the props on the Predator scrummaging machine. Telfer, the arch-scrummager, chose to overlook that plain fact.

I was selected to start the match against Natal at King's Park. This was to be played on the Saturday before the first Test. The tradition on Lions' tours was that the likely first-choice XV would have their final dress-rehearsal in such a match. The England front five were beginning to lose favour because alongside me in the front row were Keith Wood and Tom

Smith. No one could possibly argue with Woody's selection. Tom's selection at loose-head was also well-merited. He must be the quietest prop ever to play at the top level but he had proved his worth in the early matches.

So the game with Natal Sharks was my great chance. I had to keep the positives in my mind. I convinced myself that I was in with a real shout for test selection. Firstly, I and the rest of the pack had to perform. We did. The Sharks had three Springboks in their front row but we dominated them. In fact Telfer admitted afterwards that it had been the best scrummaging performance of the tour so far. We had also picked up a big win and that was a huge morale-booster seven days before the test. The only black cloud was the shoulder injury that finished Rob Howley's tour. He was heart-broken and everyone could understand why.

Whether or not I would suffer my own piece of heartache would be put on hold for three or four days until after the mid-week match against the Emerging Springboks at Wellington. I was not chosen for that game and I took that to be an encouraging sign. Jason Leonard captained the side again and Paul Wallace was on the bench. I could only conclude that the final choice for the test would lie between Paul and me. The management had told us that we would learn our fate via individual letters put under the doors of our hotel rooms. I was sharing with Jason and it was an uncomfortable feeling to know that one of us, at least, would be bitterly disappointed. The idea behind this impersonal method of notification was that it allowed us to take in the good or bad news in private.

Our letters duly arrived in the early hours of the morning and the news wasn't good. I wasn't in the test side and I wasn't on the bench. I was bitterly disappointed and, in all honesty, I couldn't understand why I had been overlooked. Jason fared little better as he was named as a replacement. Paul Wallace had leapfrogged over both of us and he was to play well in all three tests. In that respect it could be argued that the management's decision had been the correct one. I wouldn't want to take anything away from Paul and Jason and I were quick to congratulate them. It was simply that I felt that I had deserved more chances than I was given and when that chance had finally arrived against Natal I had answered all the questions asked of me.

When the realisation that I would now only feature in the remaining mid-week games had sunk in, I resolved to be as proud a Lion as ever and that I would continue to do my best in the final fortnight of the tour. As

I expected I played in both of those mid-week games and at the end I felt I could hold my head up high for my contribution. Others had equal cause to be disappointed. I was desperately sorry for Allan Bateman who, as always, showed himself to be the complete centre. Like me he had found it hard to find favour. We were the only two changes from the Natal game.

The Lions of 1997 will go down in history as a success story and for that Ian McGeechan deserves credit. His skills as a British coach were beyond question and his track record over three tours of four test victories unparalleled. From a player's point of view he was always approachable, always easy to talk to and had a wonderful demeanour. Despite my own personal disappointments I cannot deny that he had a happy team around him. He and Jim Telfer were masters of the 'good cop, bad cop' style of leadership. I'll let you guess which was which in my book. They also benefited from the example set by Fran Cotton. He was a very strong manager who was a setter of high standards in everything he did and left no one in doubt who was in charge.

The final part of the jigsaw was the captaincy of Martin Johnson. In the first place he was guaranteed a test place as he was undoubtedly one of the best lock-forwards in the business. If he had a possible weakness it was that he was a quiet guy. He knew exactly when to stand back and let others take the lead. It worked a treat.

When the dust had settled on the tour I could only reflect on my own contribution and put everything down to experience. One farcical incident reminded me that I could only laugh it off. We had attended a government reception in South Africa and been told that as we were only there for a short time we should stay off the food. Fair enough, but as time went on I, for one, was getting a tiny bit peckish. As we were finally about to leave after a social occasion far longer than had been anticipated I picked up a cocktail sausage as a small gesture towards my growing hunger. On the team coach back to our hotel I sat alongside our fitness advisor, Dave McLean.

I was not a great admirer of his because in my opinion he overdid the testing and monitoring regime which I think was purely for his own research. What is to be gained from testing players regularly on tour? He was also in charge of our hotel menus and advised us on proper eating habits. He was entitled to do that and the journey back was pleasant enough.

Imagine my surprise when some time later Geech sent for me and told me that I had been reported for eating a cocktail sausage! At first I thought he was joking but the true situation dawned on me. I was being carpeted. McLean, who had said nothing about the matter on the coach, had gone behind my back. Less than amused now, I heard the coach out and then went down to McLean's room. He refused to open the door.

In situations like that you can only laugh . . .

12

REBEL ROUSERS

The summer of 1998 will be remembered for much more than the bringing down of the final curtain on Alex Evans' career at Cardiff. As ambitious as ever, Peter Thomas and the board were actively pursuing the club's entry into ongoing cross-border competition with the English clubs. This was easier said than done because as hard as Peter and our chief executive Gareth Davies tried, obstacles were always put in their way. For all the top players and the supporters of the first-class clubs, it was crystal clear that this was exactly what the game in Wales needed. The national side had been trounced twice to the tune of over 50 points by England and France and, when we thought we couldn't sink any lower, South Africa had got within one score of the century against us.

As usual, there was much heart-searching by all concerned. The setting up of committees to look into the future of the sport would follow sooner rather than later. Peter and Gareth understandably became exasperated with the inertia and they could sense that unless something was done to improve the quality of the competition and attract the crowds the club would join a long list of others facing financial ruin. On more than one occasion it looked as if some form of Anglo-Welsh structure would be put in place but, each time, it fell at the last hurdle. Then barely a month before the new season was due to start, Gareth Davies announced that Cardiff would be playing in an unofficial Anglo-Welsh league. With him at the launch was Swansea's Roger Blyth; the good news was that the All Whites would be with us as we broke new ground.

All hell was let loose in some quarters of the game. Our English fixtures meant that the other clubs in Wales would lose their matches with the two city clubs – and, whether they were prepared to admit it or not, we were the biggest crowd-pullers and most lucrative source of gate-money wherever we went. All sorts of threats were issued, stretching from the players of Cardiff and Swansea being ineligible for the Wales squad to a lifetime ban on any referee who officiated at our matches.

This was potentially a very serious scenario for the players in particular. Yet from the outset we were genuinely excited by the prospect of playing against the best clubs in England even if it meant that we wouldn't be part of the European Cup. There was always a danger of the Welsh Rugby Union coming down heavily on us but that never materialised. We were confident that Peter Thomas had our best interests at heart and in Gareth Davies he had the ideal right-hand man. Gareth had the perfect background for his job – an international player and great club man, a spell in journalism as well as the business world, and a respected head of sport at BBC Wales before becoming the club's chief executive. Indeed a feature of what had threatened to be difficult months ahead was the way the media, with the odd exception, seemed whole-heartedly behind us in what became known as our 'rebel' season. I felt that this would possibly change as the season progressed.

One annoying feature of that season was that although there were two Welsh clubs taking this stance it was Cardiff that bore the brunt of the criticism. Swansea seemed to be travelling in our slipstream. I don't blame them for that. It was more a case of if you want someone to blame then Cardiff are the big target. A lot of the bullets were fired for the wrong reasons. I could understand the other clubs feeling aggrieved at losing our fixtures – and, no doubt, their twice-yearly attempt to put one over us on the pitch, but it was very frustrating to be accused of adopting a superior attitude towards our fellow Welsh clubs. There was no way that we were looking down at Llanelli or Pontypridd or any of the others. Peter Thomas had hoped from the outset that they would have come along with us and from what was said at the time it would appear that the Scarlets, for one, were perilously close to doing so.

What was not denied was that the English clubs would not have been interested in the first place if Cardiff were not part of an Anglo-Welsh package, so I suppose a few of our rivals in Wales put two and two together and made five. But whatever the politics of the situation the fans supported what Cardiff had done. The supporters had made it plain that they wanted something better than was previously on offer and when the season got under way the crowds flocked to the Arms Park.

TOP LEFT: Playing for Wales is a serious business . . . but really this is a happy memory of my cap for Wales Youth in 1985. The following season I took over as captain.

TOP RIGHT: Before that — and before the moustache — there had been another cause for celebration. I played four times for Wales Schools at under-15 and under-16 levels and here my grandfathers Harry George (centre) and Dave Boon share the pride I took in the achievement.

BELOW LEFT: Like father, like son. In 1987, newspaper coverage highlighted the lead I had taken from my father, Robert. As the report says, Dad had been a prop before me and had actually played at Swansea for Aberaman in a WRU Cup match.

BELOW RIGHT: A quieter moment over 20 years later. Joining Dad and myself in the family garden in Cwmdare is my youngest son, Owen.

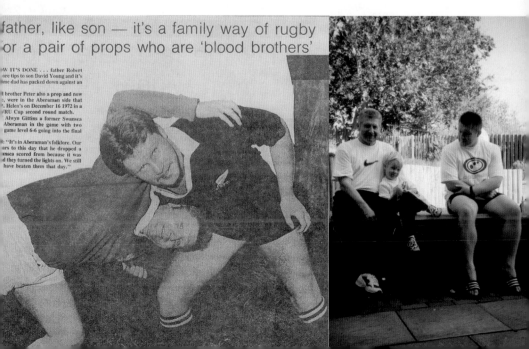

father, like son — it's a family way of rugby
or a pair of props who are 'blood brothers'

OW IT'S DONE . . . father Robert
ore tips to son David Young and it's
me dad has packed down against an

l brother Peter also a prop and now
, were in the Aberaman side that
, Helen's on December 16 1972 in a
RU Cup second round match.
Alwyn Gittins a former Swansea
Aberaman in the game with two
game level 6-6 going into the final

: "It's in Aberaman's folklore. Our
urs to this day that he dropped a
nsea scored from because it was
d they turned the lights on. We still
have beaten them that day."

ABOVE: The Welsh Lions of 1989 mark their selection in traditional manner outside the Grogg Shop in Pontypridd. Alongside me are Mike Griffiths, Ieuan Evans, Robert Jones, John Devereux and Robert Norster.

BELOW: The Lions have just beaten Australia in the second Test to level the series at one-all with one Test to play. The post-mortems begin early as I am button-holed by a local television reporter before I even reach the changing-room.

ABOVE LEFT: The camera never lies — or does it? Tony Clement and myself are shown 'signing' professional forms for Leeds Rugby League Club. Behind us are chairman Bernard Colby and coach David Ward. But those aren't league contracts that we're both signing in a stage-managed shot in readiness for the real thing a week later — by which time Clem had changed his mind.

ABOVE RIGHT: The future Mrs Young had absolutely no hesitation in approving the move to the north. April was and is a wonderful support in all aspects of my rugby career. © *Daily Mail,* Manchester

BELOW: And here I am with Colby and Ward at the press conference in Leeds. My signature is now on the real thing and my league days have begun.

ABOVE: By the time I was captain at Salford, ball-carrying and taking the ball up to the opposition was second nature to me.

BELOW: Success at Salford — as I triumphantly hold the 1995–96 First Division Championship trophy aloft. That secured the club a place in Super League.

ABOVE: Another happy gathering of rugby league players. The Wales team of 1995 had 11 former union internationals under the captaincy of Jonathan Davies. We were coached and managed by Clive Griffiths and Mike Nicholas. A year later all 11 of us had returned to the new professional game of rugby union.

BELOW LEFT: A Lion again in South Africa in 1997. If I'm not smiling it may be because of my non-selection for the Test side.

BELOW RIGHT: I'm leading the charge of the midweek team on the way to a 60-pointer against Northern Free State in the week of the final Test. Ready to support are Graham Rowntree, Nigel Redman and Tony Diprose while Tony Underwood and Rob Wainwright are grounded. © Allsport

ABOVE: Family and friends get together as Mike and Ann Griffiths and their son Luc join me and our three boys, Thomas-Rhys, Lewis and Owen.

BELOW: My first game as captain of Wales against France at the Millennium Stadium in February 2000. The other two-thirds of the front row. Garin Jenkins and Peter Rogers were great practitioners in their own right. Together we made up one of the best international units of my career. © Huw Evans Picture Agency

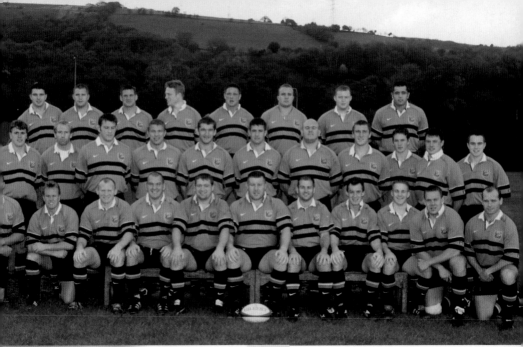

ABOVE: The Cardiff team of 1999–2000 contained its usual mix of established stars and promising youngsters. This was the season that Neil Jenkins and Craig Quinnell, amongst others, joined the club and we won the Welsh/Scottish League with three games to spare.
© Hill's Welsh Press

LEFT: My comeback game at Bedwas in January 2001 after my calf operations.
© Huw Evans Picture Agency

ABOVE: The family — my support and inspiration. April (left) sits alongside my mother, Pamela, and father, Robert. Between them are Owen and Lewis, with our eldest son, Thomas Rhys, at the front.

RIGHT: The pride of my life. Our three sports-mad sons, Lewis, Owen and Thomas-Rhys, on a family holiday in Spain in 2000 when April took them to the museum of FC Barcelona.

Our first game had been away at Bedford, not the most easily accessible place from South Wales but several hundred fans, spearheaded by half-a-dozen coaches organised by the marvellous supporters' club, had made their way to the East Midlands. That gave us a clue as to what would happen when we played our first home game the following week. Our opponents were Saracens, a club revitalised by the professional leagues in England and full of glamorous names. They all turned up for our match: Alain Penaud, Kyran Bracken, Paul Wallace, Danny Grewcock, Richard Hill and Tony Diprose. So did a 10,000-plus crowd and we then knew we were in business.

One of the great criticisms by the prophets of doom was that the English sides would field reserve teams against us as the games were not important to them. Nothing could have been further from the truth for two-thirds of that season. Against Northampton I found myself propping against the Springbok loose-head Garry Pagel; after that it was Kevin Yates of Bath and the Canadian international Harry Toews at Leicester. Some reserves!

The other criticism from outside was that the whole experiment collapsed after Christmas. I didn't see that, either. Our return match with Saracens in mid-January featured the same opposition as at the start of the season, with new names like Paddy Johns added to the opposition pack, and when we went to Bath a month later a capacity crowd turned up to see a near full-strength home team. That match was a perfect example of the meaningfulness of the project. Our home fixture against the West Country side in October, had all the 'bite' and niggle that any official competition could hope to generate.

That match will be remembered for the sending-off of Bath's international prop Victor Ubogu in the dying moments of the first half. Once again the Arms Park was packed to the rafters, and there were many others on rooftops, the balconies of the Westgate Street flats and the banking alongside the river at the west end of the ground. They had their money's worth with a pulsating match highlighted in the first half by a brilliant individual try by Rob Howley. Bath had disputed the legality of that and the temperature had already risen when the referee, Alun Ware, penalised Ubogu for dissent. Victor then swore at him and was sent off. He was reluctant to leave the field and moments later the half-time whistle went. Then the fun and games started.

In the tunnel under the main stand Bath's coach, Andy Robinson, was incensed. Ubogu was protesting his innocence (several Cardiff players were in a good position to say otherwise). Robinson was going on at great length about biased refereeing and what he saw as a string of unfair penalties against his side. Actually the first-half penalty-count against both sides was neck and neck until Victor's comments and in the second period the penalties against us finished at 9–2.

For several minutes it looked as if there wouldn't be a second half as Robinson refused to let his side leave the changing-room. All sorts of committee-men and officials were gathering in the vicinity but I went to see Andy and his captain, Andy Nichol, and suggested that we all calm down. Fortunately everyone did and we went back out for Cardiff to win the game in the final quarter with two more top-notch tries, from Gareth Thomas and Mike Rayer.

The post-match reaction, however, was less pleasing with the focus of attention being the quality of the refereeing. The critics saw this as a heaven-sent opportunity to broaden the issue from the particular events of the game with Bath to the standard of refereeing in all the rebel games. After the initial threat by the Welsh Rugby Union and the Rugby Football Union in England to ban any referee who officiated at our games, a small group of referees agreed to come forward. All but one of them was Welsh and they were perfectly competent. They received a major boost as the season was getting under way when Fred Howard, an Englishman, joined them. He was one of the top men of his generation having handled 20 internationals all over the world, including two World Cups. There was no arguing with his pedigree. Later in the season when he controlled our match with Swansea in front of another capacity crowd at St Helen's he gave one of the best exhibitions of sympathetic but firm refereeing you could ever hope to see. (And I say that even though he sent two of our pack to the sin-bin and reduced us to 13 men!)

In some respects they were easy targets because they were not the 'big names'. They were, nevertheless, fully-qualified and had satisfied the standards of the Welsh Rugby Union for several seasons. One thing I noticed was that as they were now outside the fold and didn't have the assessors that were normally sent to league and cup matches, they seemed more relaxed. The use of referees' assessors is a double-edged sword. You are left with the uneasy feeling that our top referees are out there in the middle knowing that they are being watched and perhaps subconsciously controlling the game according to some predetermined format.

The turning point for Cardiff in the rebel season, both in terms of the fall-out for the club internally and the preparation for the remaining matches, was our disastrous defeat in the semi-final of the Welsh Cup. By one of those quirks of Welsh rugby politics it had been conceded by those in power that although Cardiff and Swansea were no longer part of the Welsh Premier League they were still eligible for the cup competition. It didn't take too much of an imagination to realise that somewhere along the line the cup's sponsors Swalec had put their foot down, insisting that both clubs were to be included. The competition was to be meaningful and attractive, from a business as well as a sporting point of view.

Whatever went on behind the scenes, the Union accepted that we should take part – with one proviso. Whereas all of the senior clubs only came into the cup in the later rounds, Cardiff and Swansea would have to play their way through from round one. We had no problems with that and we had some great occasions, starting in our very first tie when the famous rugby league wing Anthony Sullivan made his debut for us at Cilfynydd. Ian Botham had a pie and a pint in the local pub before standing on the grassy bank to watch his son Liam notch a hat-trick of tries for us. If ever there was a case of 'the romance of the cup' this was it. Then we played Seven Sisters, Llandovery and Abertillery before winning at Aberavon and Pontypool. We had already played six rounds of cup ties before coming up against Llanelli in the semi-final at Bridgend. I don't think any of us fully appreciated the hidden agenda behind this particular match.

Here was the classic encounter made for the headline writers. Wicked Cardiff who, allegedly, had turned their back on the Welsh game and their responsibilities within it, up against the cavaliers from Llanelli, who played rugby of the gods and had stayed loyal to sport in their homeland. It was a load of old cobblers, of course, but we knew that was how some people saw it. What I remember with affection about our rebel season was that, despite what was being said about us in certain sections of the press and by the die-hard supporters of the other clubs, our friendships with and mutual respect for the players outside Cardiff and Swansea were unaffected. You don't turn away from the likes of Scott Quinnell, Rupert Moon and Robin McBryde overnight. If anything, whenever we met at national squad sessions and elsewhere, they were genuinely interested in how we were getting on at club level and, often, envious of the quality of rugby we were enjoying.

Even so, it was a different scenario when Cardiff played Llanelli for the only time that year. What happened that day at the Brewery Field is still hard to believe – and I'm not talking about the fact that we were undoubtedly well beaten. The business of us being 'rebels' who had betrayed Wales was blown up out of all proportion. The hostility towards the entire Cardiff team, their officials and their supporters was unprecedented, in my experience. Forget Wales v England or the Lions in Australia in 1989 or Salford in a local derby at Wigan or Warrington, this was ugly – really ugly. All East–West matches are keen and all cup semi-finals are intense and, yes, perhaps we underestimated the intensity and physicality that the Scarlets would bring into the game. But there was something more driving them forward that day. The traditional edge to a game against the 'city slickers', some might call it envy, had reached an unparalleled new level.

The reasons why Cardiff had chosen to play the English clubs had been misunderstood – and misquoted – in some quarters all season and matters came to the boil at the Brewery Field. It was not so much what went on in the game itself because it was a typical cup tie. Llanelli were fired up and they played really well. Scott Quinnell is a magnificent game-breaker and he was in his element in a rampant pack in which Mike Voyle and Chris Wyatt were outstanding. Yet we started well and led by ten points after a quarter of an hour. Then everything went haywire. Rob Howley was sin-binned for deliberately killing possession at a scrum on our own line and then Derwyn Jones followed him for illegal use of his feet in a ruck. By then four penalty goals had wiped out our lead and there was an air of unreality about the whole proceedings.

We didn't know it at the time but several members of the Cardiff board and committee had been the targets of verbal abuse in the grandstand and heaven knows what our loyal supporters were enduring on the terraces. On that particular day it seemed that the frustrations of every fan outside the Cardiff club were vented on us. It was a thoroughly unpleasant experience. In the end we were well beaten with Llanelli scoring three tries. We were dejected and knew we had let ourselves down but, even so, were shocked by what happened next.

Before the next week was out Terry Holmes had given notice of his resignation as head coach with effect from the end of the season. This was a tragedy for Terry and for the club. There was speculation that he may have been pushed but his public stance remained consistent to the end. He said that Cardiff had made the right decision in setting up fixtures with the English clubs but he was disappointed that as the end of the season approached there was already talk of both Cardiff and Swansea returning to the Welsh League. Terry couldn't agree with that and he posed the valid question of whether we had wasted a year. He had decided to step back from coaching and give more time to his business interests.

Terry was understandably dejected but the team still believed in what Peter Thomas had tried to set up. It was equally true that our admiration for Terry was unshakeable. He understood Cardiff rugby through and through and it was a sad day six weeks later when we played our final Anglo-Welsh match and Terry walked away from the club. With him went great Cardiff stalwarts – team manager, Peter Manning, who was already at Cardiff when I first arrived at the club back in 1988, the assistant coaches, Hemi Taylor and Mark Ring, and sadly, my mentor Charlie Faulkner.

It was a flat end to what had started out as a visionary experiment – but deep down we all accepted that the novelty had worn off. After the cup defeat we had five matches left and a couple of the English clubs sent academy sides to the Arms Park. We beat Newcastle by 70 points and playing almost unopposed rugby racked up 96 points against Richmond. That was not what we had gone into England for and it was time to call it a day.

Every one of us, however, knew that the establishment of an official Anglo-Welsh or, better still, British League had to be a priority for the game in Wales and in the British Isles.

13

THE REDEEMER COMETH

I first met Graham Henry at the National Sports Centre in Sophia Gardens, Cardiff. Ironically, it was the same venue where the Wales squad had prepared for internationals under the direction of Kevin Bowring. This, however, was a different scene altogether. Our new coach had been brought from the other side of the world. He had an impressive track record with Auckland Blues and he had, it was reported, endangered any chance in the future of coaching the All Blacks by coming to Wales.

From the moment he walked into the room he had what can only be described as a 'Readybrek' glow about him. There was an almost indefinable air of quiet confidence in the man. He was with Terry Cobner but he asked for no introductions. He had never spoken to us before but he knew Rob Howley, Scott Gibbs, Neil Jenkins and me. We were considered the senior players and he had asked to meet us for an informal chat over a cup of coffee.

He threw in a few questions and then sat back and listened to the answers. They ranged from the general, 'What has gone well . . . What has disappointed you?' to the personal, 'How are you feeling . . . Are you looking forward to the internationals?' He built up a rapport with us while still giving us the impression that this was not just a leisurely chat that would mean nothing in the long run. It was an impressive start. We were to learn quite quickly that Graham is always prepared to listen but will always tell you if he thinks you are wrong. Graham is always the first to congratulate you on your performance but is not afraid to tell you if he thinks you have fallen short of the standards he expects either on training or playing fields. No one is ever in any doubt who is in charge.

He left us excited about what lay ahead. His parting message to us was: 'You must aim to be number one in your position in the world, not Wales . . .'

Graham went to meet the rugby and fitness coaches of the first-class clubs to give a brief outline on his rugby philosophy and the fitness standards he was hoping to obtain, and with them, as with us, he listened. The time was fast approaching for these ideas to be put into practice.

I am often asked why Graham Henry came to Wales to become national coach and the answer is that I don't really know. What I do know is that he is not afraid of a challenge. I hope it's not too much of a cliché to say that he's a 'man's man'. That is certainly what he is. Everyone in Welsh rugby, including the officials and committee-men, quickly came to realise that he's not afraid to confront issues even if it means the occasional important nose is put very much out of joint.

What proved very much in his favour in his first three years was that having gained the support and trust of the players they delivered some success on the field. We realised from an early stage that although he was a talker – quite a talker – he was also very much a doer. The results in the first season earned him the infamous tag, 'The Great Redeemer', the origins of which lay in a poster campaign from the WRU's own office. I'm sure it was the sort of title that Graham could have done without, for the 1999 World Cup was barely a year away and time was not on his side.

It is even now difficult to appreciate the task confronting him in his first few months. He had an international with South Africa to prepare for, again at Wembley, and somehow had to repair the psychological damage inflicted by the Springboks' near-100 point trouncing of us the previous summer. That had been admittedly against a weakened Wales team but coming after the half-century by France, it had done nothing to build our confidence as a rugby nation.

What Graham did was restore our self-belief. I will never forget his team-talk before that Springbok match. I had been selected for the game only to be sidelined by a knee ligament injury playing for Cardiff the previous Saturday, but he had insisted that I went along with the team. It was Graham's intention to keep all players involved even when sidelined by injury. There were several signs that all the players had responded to his methods in the previous two months. More than anything we all *wanted* to be part of the new regime. That had not always been the case in the past. The intensity of what he said at Wembley was incredible. Even as an onlooker on that occasion I realised that he was the best pre-match motivational speaker I had heard. His public statements were designed to play down expectations but behind closed doors he left none of the team in any doubt that they were capable of success. He told each player what was expected of him and that he was capable of achieving it.

The coach was by no means a one-man band. He had assembled around him an impressive management team. This was not something he had rushed into. There had been meetings and he had taken time to reflect on what he had heard. Eventually he announced that Lynn Howells would be his assistant coach – this was ten months before Lynn became head coach at Cardiff. I was pleased for Lynn because he had worked his way up to the top through the various representative sides while continuing as Dennis John's right-hand man at the Pontypridd club. The two of them had taken Wales to South Africa after Kevin Bowring's departure. They had been given a thankless 'caretaker' role with a weakened side and as well as being humiliated 13–96 in the test they had lost the four provincial games as well. John had now returned to coaching the Wales A side and it must have been a huge confidence booster for Lynn Howells to be asked to carry on with Graham. He knew he would be on a big learning curve.

The team manager was David Pickering, a former captain of Wales who fitted into Graham's image of a modern, professional squad. 'Dai Pick', as he was known to all of us, had valuable experience in the world of business and he got to grips with sorting out the players' contracts. This was one of the issues that Graham wanted settled sooner rather than later. He had listened to our comments about the excessive amount of training caused by the twin demands of club and country. He agreed there was no need for centralised training three times a week. The employment of development officers who were international players on a retainer had become unworkable in his opinion. Only seven of the twenty-two players involved in the match with France at Wembley were employed in those jobs. The system had become unfair because a dozen or so players who had been given the jobs were no longer in the national team. So they were abolished and on one hand I was happy to see them go because as with any dual contract system the players always find themselves stuck in the middle, but on the other hand we were losing a guaranteed amount of money. Under the new contracts, it was a purely pay for play system where the player received remuneration after playing in a game. A player could take part in every squad training session but if he did not run out on the day of the game he received nothing. This is hard as a great deal of hard work and preparation goes on throughout the season which could be worth nothing financially in the end. The management felt that this structure would add to the hunger of the players, perhaps giving us more edge.

As with the rest of the back-room staff, Pickering was charged with the responsibility of creating a positive squad atmosphere. He – and they – certainly succeeded for that first 18 months was the happiest time I had ever known at that level. There was also Trevor James, as squad manager continuing in the role he had started in 1996.

All of these people complemented each other perfectly as a management team and the icing on the cake was provided by someone who was the most unusual appointment of all. A new fitness coach was needed after Dave Clark had left to allow Graham to choose his own man. That turned out to be Steve Black, a Geordie who seemed to have done everything from acting and wrestling to helping Newcastle United at soccer and Newcastle Falcons at rugby. All of which says absolutely nothing about the character of the loveable newcomer who was about to come into our lives.

Blackie is a one-off. When I saw him for the first time I couldn't believe his appearance. He was big, which is another way of saying he was probably overweight, and he was our fitness coach! He has no problems with that because he jokes about it himself. His task was to make us and not himself fitter and stronger. In no time at all I realised that every one of the national squad had a new friend for life, a father figure who was totally positive and totally supportive. He once said to me, 'If you have any worries and think I can help, ring me at any time. Don't worry if it's two o'clock in the morning and you want to do a bit of extra training – call me and I'll be there!'

For Blackie, the players always came first and his training schedules were always based on the needs of the individual. If a player turned up for training feeling low, perhaps because of a domestic crisis or something else totally unrelated to rugby, Blackie was the first person I met who accepted that rugby players were only human beings and they did experience problems outside which affected them. Blackie knew that at times like these he would be better served sitting down and having a chat over a cup of coffee to help sort things out. The hard graft could come later. Two years down the road his methods would be used as a stick to beat him with but from day one they worked with the Wales squad. The weariness and boredom went out of the window. He did away with fitness tests because he said they created potential and unnecessary pressure for the players and the success of his methods was based on relaxation. 'We work hard and we laugh hard!' summed up his approach.

He didn't underestimate the need for stamina but speed and reaction were equally important and he had a range of drills to help us achieve them. In my own case he realised that I had suffered a few injuries and had been playing at the top level for 12 years so he changed my training to shorter sessions that took the pressure off my joints. He convinced me that I was on the right road to a longer playing career, and for that and a lot more, I am in his debt and always will be.

Needless to say, when Graham Henry was in full flow in pre-match pep talks, Blackie was invariably at his side, the perfect partner as they built up our confidence. He would be perpetually in motion, going from one player to another with quiet words of encouragement. Both of them had the knack of saying the right thing at the right time. Graham must spend hours watching videos and analysing the strengths and weaknesses of the opposition because we certainly do not start any game unprepared. Every Welsh player knows his role and the game plan for that day. We didn't quite beat South Africa at Wembley, slipping behind in the dying moments after a heroic team performance. I had watched from the stand and even in defeat could see that this time we might be turning the corner at last. There was dejection in the changing-room afterwards because history had been staring the team in the face – Wales had never beaten the Springboks – but Graham's first words were, 'You've earned the right to hold your heads up high . . . we will go on from this to something even better.' Then he and Blackie sat down with the players and had a beer. From that moment on we were all much closer.

The funny thing was that although the togetherness of the squad was almost infectious, not everything went according to plan for me. I was still unable to play in the next match against Argentina at Llanelli and, worse still, when we went up to play Scotland in the first game of that season's Five Nations Championship I pulled a calf muscle and was forced to withdraw. I was heartbroken because I wanted so much to be part of what was going on. I flew home and watched the game on television. A fortnight later I played at last, but I was probably unwise to do so. It was against Ireland at Wembley and with the calf still playing me up it was really a case of playing on one leg. I made the decision to play after Graham had privately told me that he felt that the team needed me to play this game but at the same time he understood that I was not 100 per cent. What was equally worrying was that Wales had lost both games. Had the Henry bubble burst? If he had any self-doubt he didn't show it and continued to talk us up as we came through what threatened to be a mini-crisis.

I was uncertain, however, about the part I would play in the remainder of the season. I told Graham that my calf needed a long rest if it was to recover properly. 'Let's give it a week or two,' he replied, 'and see how you feel then.' Wales went without me to Paris and enjoyed a sensational win over a shell-shocked France. The team were also due to play a friendly match against Italy in Treviso. A full month had elapsed since the Irish match and it seemed an ideal time to return. The pain in my leg had cleared up and Graham suggested that I should have a run-out in the A match on the Friday evening in Rovigo. I won't pretend that I was wildly enthusiastic about the idea. Apart from anything else I think such matches should be used as stepping-stones for youngsters on the way up, not as trial matches for old war horses with 40 caps under their belt. Nevertheless I played in a game that promised to be a not too arduous run-out for me. It didn't quite work out like that. With an inexperienced French referee turning a blind eye, the Italians kicked seven bells out of us. They also kicked a lot of penalties and beat us by a point.

The only consolation was that I had proved my fitness and I was back in the 22-man squad for what turned out to be a marvellous win over England at Wembley. I was called on as a replacement for the final 15 minutes and shared in the jubilation after Scott Gibbs' last-ditch try and Neil Jenkins' match-winning conversion. We had shown guts and determination to hang on in a match that England should have sewn up long before those final scenes. We had every reason to celebrate but it was equally important to keep our feet on the ground. We had finished the season on an unbelievable high but the World Cup was only five months away and before that we had a summer tour to Argentina. And I was still not an automatic choice for selection at prop.

14

REBELS NO MORE

Cardiff returned to the Welsh fold in the summer of 1999. The coach appointed to take over from Terry Holmes was Lynn Howells. This was an interesting appointment because Lynn had gradually worked his way through the national coaching set-up to be appointed as assistant to Graham Henry with the Wales squad. We all realised that he was talking on a demanding responsibility at the club because he had been an assistant to Dennis John at Pontypridd as well as Henry's right-hand man. However, about a dozen of the Cardiff squad knew of Lynn's capabilities first-hand. He had done a good job as forwards' coach for Wales and there had been whispers in the squad for a few months that he was looking for a bigger role at club level. Lynn is one of the nice guys in rugby and I was confident that he would make a lot of new friends at Cardiff. The nagging doubt was whether he could adjust quickly to becoming number one – we were back to the old problem of Cardiff wanting instant remedies and success.

One of the first things Lynn did was meet me to ask if I would carry on as club captain. He felt sure we could work well together and I had no reason to doubt him. Twelve months earlier Terry Holmes and Charlie Faulkner had persuaded me to assume the captaincy by stressing what an honour the post was at Cardiff. They had done that by insisting that I study the board in the clubhouse listing the past captains. I couldn't deny that I would be following a long line of great players. I told them frankly that what worried me were two things: the huge responsibility that I would be taking on, and all the off-the-field expectations that would understandably go hand-in-hand with such a prestigious position. If you are a Gerald Davies or a Bob Norster, both celebrated public speakers, the social side of the role came naturally. I would have to work at it. I think Terry and Charlie knew exactly what I meant by that but I am indebted to them to this day for convincing me that I was equal to the task.

I had enjoyed my first year and it didn't take me long to accept Lynn's invitation to carry on. I didn't regret it one bit. With any new coach there are always comings and goings. He had brought in a new coaching team with Geraint John as his assistant and Bob Norster returned to the fold as team manager. Sadly a former playing colleague, Huw Bevan, who had retired to be Cardiff's fitness coach, and had done an excellent job for a year, was released from his position to make way for Lynn to appoint his own man. I would say that under Huw the squad's fitness as a whole had improved and I think I am right in saying that all the squad were disappointed to see him leave as we had enjoyed working with him. The new man appointed by Lynn was Huw Wiltshire. Huw, a senior lecturer at UWIC, settled to his task and immediately struck up a great relationship with all the players. I feel that I have been lucky to work with two of the best fitness coaches in Wales and owe them both a great deal as they have worked closely with me when I have been recovering from injury.

Somehow a depleted squad saw the club through the first two months of the season when many of us, including Lynn, were away with the Wales team for the World Cup. That was a particularly difficult time because although we were focused on the internationals our minds inevitably turned to what was going on at the club. Several new players had joined the club, including Neil Jenkins, Nick Walne, Mike Voyle, Craig Quinnell and Martyn Williams, but the World Cup kept them away until the end of October. Lynn pulled a master stroke in the preseason build-up when he insisted that all of the World Cup players who had a day off from the Wales camp travel with the rest of the Cardiff squad for a Sunday afternoon friendly at Bristol. That did us all the world of good. We couldn't play, of course, but just for the likes of Neil and the others to be there sitting in the stand and identified as Cardiff players was an important step. The club's travelling support saw them, the autograph hunters mingled with them in relaxed surroundings and, most importantly of all, the boys felt part of their new club.

When we rejoined the squad two months later, we found everyone in good heart, not least because after a shaky start they had won five and drawn one of their eight league games and given us a strong position from which to challenge for the title. With several players on short-term contracts my vice-captain, Mike Rayer, and the assistant coach Geraint

John had done a superb job and it was no mean achievement in our first year together that we went another 16 matches unbeaten in the inaugural Welsh/Scottish League to finish as champions.

That was followed by another season, in 2000–01, when we finished second to Swansea in the league, but whatever we did in domestic competition paled into insignificance alongside our mixed fortunes in Europe. Some people will say that Cardiff made a rod for their own back by signing players with the stated intention of building a squad to win the Heineken Cup. There is no point in denying that at different times in different places leading spokesmen have said exactly that. But two or three years down the road we have all learnt to be a bit more circumspect. That's not because we think we can't win it but more a case of realising that the standard of rugby has become incredibly high – as we all want it to be – and to win you need ability but also a degree of luck.

We are criticised in Wales for our alleged attempts to 'buy' success with big name signings. We would all do well to remember that players like Josh Kronfeld, Ian Jones, Jason Little, Pat Howard, Olivier Brouzet and Thomas Castaignede have been drafted into the top English clubs in recent seasons to strengthen their chances in Europe. A club like Leicester Tigers has done well because it has integrated the newcomers with the talent within the club. Thankfully, Cardiff has come to realise this and is now actively promoting a policy whereby young players in the Cardiff youth team stay with the club, firstly with the newly established under-21 squad, and then are introduced gradually to first-team rugby.

Sometimes they graduate sooner rather than later. The best examples were Rhys Williams and Jamie Robinson who virtually rocketed out of youth rugby. Rhys won his first Wales cap after only 16 games of senior rugby and shone against Ireland in Dublin. Jamie had to wait a bit longer but benefited from a demanding season of 30 appearances for the first team, before touring Japan and winning his cap a couple of months after his twenty-first birthday. Alongside them in the club squad at the end of the 2000–01 season were a dozen other players not yet 22 years old, including Ryan and Gary Powell and Owain Ashman, and the signs were that even more youngsters would be joining them.

By September 2001, I was ready to start my fourth year as captain – and under my third coach in that time. Lynn Howells had announced that he was not seeking an extension to his two-year contract. Lynn's stated objective had been to make Cardiff more consistent and I don't think anyone could argue that his goals were achieved in that area. The board of directors turned to South Africa and appointed Rudy Joubert, from Boland, as director of rugby. I met Rudy soon after his arrival and agreed to carry on as captain.

It is well known that after my playing days are over I want to stay in rugby and pursue a career in coaching, perhaps giving back a little of what I have learnt over the years. I have tried to learn something new from each of the coaches I have worked with. Along the way I have tried to put some of this into practice and I was very fortunate in 1998 when one of my local clubs, Abercynon, invited me to help out at their training sessions. It started out as one session but, as they say, one thing led to another. The club was in good hands with Robert Downes, who had played youth rugby with me, coaching the backs and Paul Efford, the forwards. They had a marvellous rapport with their players and I learned a lot by simply watching them. I contributed a couple of hours, input and thanked them for the opportunity. It didn't end there – both men were due to go on their annual holiday and they asked if I would be prepared to step in and cover for them. On their return from holiday, Robert Paul and the chairman, Gordon Williams, asked me to come on board on a more permanent basis as the players had enjoyed my sessions. Robert and Paul felt that we worked well together and we could learn from each other.

I couldn't refuse their request and, frankly, I didn't want to. I was chuffed to bits to think I could put something back into the game at a local level. The only thing I had to be careful of was to balance my new enthusiasm for coaching with my playing career and the captaincy of Cardiff, which would unquestionably continue to take priority. For several months everything worked out very well. I went along to Abercynon every Tuesday and Thursday evening and became increasingly involved in hands-on coaching. If Cardiff didn't have a match on a Saturday then I could go again and see at first hand how the team was playing; if not, I would be given a video of their game to analyse.

An unexpected benefit of this arrangement was that I was able to bring along some Cardiff players who, for various reasons were not getting enough rugby, to play for Abercynon. Both Steve Moore, an international lock who was recovering from a serious knee injury, and Phil Wheeler, a promising flanker who had made a big impression for Wales Schools, welcomed the chance to play there. An even better example was the young wing, Craig Morgan, who was desperately short of match practice at one point. He had made a big impression when he first played senior rugby as an 18-year-old but had lost a bit of confidence after a knee injury. The bracing air of Abercynon did wonders for Craig! He played several games for them and his running in midfield was devastating. To his great credit he wholeheartedly embraced the idea of regaining his form at what some players would see as a second-class club. I was able to monitor his progress and report back to Lynn Howells. When the time came for him to return to the Arms Park he left behind an army of friends in the valley and to this day they follow his progress at the top level. They've had plenty to follow because Craig showed exceptional form for Cardiff, scoring tries in 17 consecutive matches, including a couple of spectacular length-of-the-field efforts. He is undoubtedly one of the richest talents to play for the club for several years and it is only a matter of time before he wins his cap.

The objective at Abercynon in my first season with them was to protect a position in Division Two as they had been relegated the previous year. As things worked out we were promoted to Division One of the Welsh League and we did that as champions with only six defeats in 26 matches. The challenge in the following year would be to stay there and that couldn't be taken for granted. Inevitably there was a greater intensity at the club in that second season for me and I soon realised that their expectations of me were, understandably, increasing. In the opening months of the new season I was in all but name their director of rugby. I found myself doing far more than on the field, coaching twice a week. I was sorting out contracts, managing a budget, overseeing fitness training and providing game plans for matches I wouldn't see first hand. It was invaluable experience that, if all goes to plan, I will one day put to good use. With my Cardiff and Wales commitments still at the very top of my priorities there were simply not enough hours in the day.

By Christmas I knew I would, with great reluctance, have to step down at the end of the season. The team manager, Jeff Howells, who had helped me considerably had also resigned so it seemed the right time for Abercynon to have a new duo guiding them. Luckily, two players reaching the end of their first-class careers were available to fill the gaps. Phil John and Mark Rowley had been magnificent servants of the Pontypridd club for several years and they agreed to take over the reins further up the valley – and Abercynon stayed in Division One as they had aimed to do. Although disappointed to leave the helm of Abercynon I knew that I had left them in a strong position in the league and financially they were secure.

We had parted on good terms and I am still in contact with them. My 18 months with Abercynon had confirmed in my own mind that my future lies in coaching, an ambition that has been further strengthened by the two national coaches I have been fortunate enough to work with since my return to rugby union.

15

THE WORLD CUP

I knew before we went that the trip to Argentina could be make-or-break time for me. Having beaten Italy, France and England the team was on a roll and it couldn't be taken for granted that I would win my place back. The matches out there would mark the beginning of the final run-in to the World Cup in Wales in the autumn and the time for experimenting was nearly over. The Wales team had already developed a settled look.

Graham Henry put things in a nutshell when he sat down with me after the first Test in Buenos Aires and asked, 'Do you want it enough?' He said that early on he had become as guilty as previous coaches of giving me the impression that Wales could not be successful without me – my experience was invaluable if the team was to be a success. He also asked me if I felt that I was an automatic choice when fit. He explained the question by saying that when he had first arrived he was aware that there was a limited choice on selection but he had come to realise that there were other options after Ben Evans had played well in good victories.

'It' was the number three jersey in the Wales pack for the great challenges that were just around the corner. My answer simply had to be 'Yes' and 'No'. I would never take my selection for granted and I knew that I had to prove myself again to regain my place. I could sense that Graham was probing to test my reaction as well as my answer. He needed to be convinced that I was utterly determined to become first choice again and I think I succeeded. The day before, Wales had beaten the Pumas and Ben Evans of Swansea had played at tight-head prop. Ben and his club mate Chris Anthony had by then started in seven of the eight internationals that had been played since Henry had taken over. The situation was unlikely to change for the second Test with Argentina a week later. I had been called on for the final 20 minutes in the first Test and would sit on the bench again for the next one. My realistic target for selection had to be the match with South Africa that would open the Millennium Stadium at the end of June.

The Argentinian tour had been a success and after a short break the entire squad assembled again at our base at the Copthorne Hotel on the outskirts of Cardiff. We would now be together nearly all the time up to the opening of the World Cup on 1 October. This was a prolonged preparation by an international side that was unique in my experience. We were scheduled to play three full tests and a non-cap match against the USA Eagles, all at the new stadium, in the space of five weeks that summer and the management team were leaving no stone unturned in their efforts to identify their strongest line-up.

I knew that the team selected for the South African match would be the one that gave the best clue to Henry's thinking and that if it did well, or even won, it was unlikely that he would look any further for his World Cup team. To my delight and great relief I got the nod over Ben Evans, who was on the bench, and Chris Anthony and from then on things could hardly have gone better.

It was hard to believe that after two seasons' travel to Wembley to play our home matches we were finally back in Cardiff. The Millennium Stadium was still not finished and there were only nine weeks before the opening ceremony of the World Cup. Yet the conviction of the WRU's chairman, Glanmor Griffiths, was almost willing everything to be ready on time. He needed the summer internationals to be played there to gradually increase the size of the crowd and obtain all the necessary safety certificates. Whether the team needed so many games was another matter but once our preparations were under way the whys and wherefores never entered our minds. We were entirely focused on playing and beating South Africa for the first time ever. And we did.

It was a complete team performance that afternoon and one that made everyone realise that Graham Henry's long-term strategy for the national team was paying dividends. We had been lucky to beat England at Wembley, though we made our own luck on the day, and we had been careless in the two tests in Argentina but still deserved to win both. The match with the Springboks, however, was on a different plane altogether. We were aided by an outstanding playing surface that stood up well to the heavy rain in the second half and buoyed up by a fantastic atmosphere at the stadium. It was hard to believe that only 29,000 fans had been allowed into the unfinished ground because they made a noise more like three times their number. We played the controlled rugby that all the coaching for the previous year had been geared towards. Our set piece play was outstanding and Mark Taylor and Gareth Thomas scored tries that were perfect examples of how to maximise every opportunity. When the Springboks threw everything into attack in the third quarter our defence was magnificent, and the only disappointment was that we let them score a try late in the game that brought the final score back to 29–19. But we had won and nothing could alter that fact. Graham Henry and the entire management team joined us on the pitch at the end of the match and as he broke away with Rob Howley to give press interviews Lynn Howells and Blackie walked around the touch-line trying to take it all in. It was a moment to savour and they deserved it.

The later games against Canada and France were equally important in the overall build-up to the World Cup and it was important that we kept winning. I played in the French match that ended 34–23 in our favour with Neil Jenkins finishing with 29 points of his own, including 9 penalty goals. After years of unfair criticism and uncertainty Neil was benefiting from a coach who had complete faith in him. The Ginger Monster responded with a series of performances that amounted to far more than his impeccable goal-kicking. He was running the show from fly-half with tactical kicks and superb passing. He had endured a nightmare game (like most of us) when France had run up their half-century at Wembley but that ghost had well and truly been laid to rest. He had been outstanding when Wales won in Paris, surprising the opposition with his clean breaks and readiness to run, and now he had won against them again. In those two games in 1999 he had scored 48 points – a good way of wiping the 0–51 slate clean.

With the summer matches out of the way, the Wales squad hit the road. A training camp was organised for Portugal in early September and, before that, we travelled around Wales calling at towns that had seen nothing like it before. Wherever we went in Mid- and North Wales big crowds turned up to watch us train. Too often in the past rugby was seen as the game of the south but for several years it had been gathering new fans in the north. Anyone who had been to our internationals at Wembley would have seen dozens of coaches from Caernarvon and Bangor and Wrexham in the coach park there. The fans had been able to obtain far more tickets than normal and they had been great supporters. Now we were taking the Wales team to them.

This was great but it only served to heighten the expectations already heaped on our shoulders. Graham knew it was almost impossible to dampen this optimism but when we saw the smiling faces everywhere and when we signed the hundreds of autographs at every stopover it was hard not to feel part of something special. But could we win the World Cup? The victory over South Africa had shown that we were an improving side but we knew that if we were to have any chance we would have to take our game up yet another level.

Blackie was a wonderful motivator in the long, final month of September but time still dragged. All around us the media hype continued. I couldn't help thinking how things had changed since the first World Cup back in 1987. It seemed a world away now. When I had been called up to Brisbane from my summer of club rugby in Canberra the atmosphere was hardly that of a major sports festival. Outside Wales the fact that we had reached the semi-final and then finished third meant little. In the years in between the tournament had undoubtedly grown and it had done so without any contribution from Wales. We had failed to go any further than the pool matches in two consecutive World Cups and world rugby was threatening to leave us behind.

I had missed those two tournaments while I was playing rugby league. Ironically, I was part of a World Cup campaign that was far more successful for Wales – staged by the league authorities in 1995. It would be foolish to pretend that it was staged on anything like the scale of even the first union tournament and yet it captured the imagination of the success-starved rugby fans of Wales. Whether it was by accident or by design that 1995 championship could not have come at a better time. All the ex-union stars were still in league and it was a heaven-sent opportunity for us to get together as a team. It was a bit like an old pop group joining up for a reunion tour. There were so many of us that a Wales rugby league team had already been re-formed in 1991 and we had won several matches, including an 18–16 defeat of England. The games had mostly been played at the Vetch Field in Swansea or Ninian Park in Cardiff but they had attracted 10,000-plus crowds.

So it was a natural development to enter a Wales team in the World Cup, with the added attraction of playing both our first round matches in South Wales. All the players loved the idea and we were genuinely excited about playing rugby, even if it was the league version, in our own backyard. We were a team of good mates and we were a proud camp. We also had a bit of ability. The former union players alone included Allan Bateman, Scott Gibbs, Jonathan Davies, John Devereux, Adrian Hadley,

Jonathan Griffiths and Kevin Ellis in the backs and Scott Quinnell, Mark Jones, Paul Moriarty, Rowland Phillips, Richard Webster and me in the pack. Throw in some pedigree league men like Anthony Sullivan, Richard Eyres, Kelvin Skerrett, Keiron Cunningham and the precocious talent of the 18-year-old Iestyn Harris and you have quite a team!

The influence of our coach, Clive Griffiths, was exceptional. He had single-handedly put the squad together and he was delighted with our success. The seeds had been sown by Jim Mills and Mike Nicholas and Clive carried on their good work. Griffiths was a disciplinarian but not one who imposed curfews. Perhaps we would have benefited from a few more restrictions because we didn't play well in our first match against France. To put it mildly we had enjoyed a week of serious socialising, finding it hard to break away from good company and the growing army of well-wishers in the city centre of Cardiff.

But we beat France and then knuckled down for the much greater threat posed by Western Samoa in our next match at the Vetch. It was a great occasion with over 15,000 fans – many of them leading figures on the rugby union committees – packed into the ground. It was the most physical game I have ever played in, with some ferocious tackling. By the end I felt as if my shirt was full of loose ribs but it was worth it. We had won again to qualify for a semi-final against England and I had been voted man-of-the-match.

Time for serious socialising, part two. The semi-final was to be played at Old Trafford in Manchester a week later and we were given the option of travelling north immediately or staying in Cardiff until 48 hours before the match. You can guess what we chose. With the excitement growing, we had a whale of a time for a couple of days and then settled down to the task ahead. We felt we had a real chance against England, although we were the underdogs. If we couldn't play in Wales then Old Trafford was the next best venue. Everything about the place – the facilities, the pitch, changing-rooms – reeks of class. And on that day in particular the stands and terraces became a sea of red: the red of Wales, not Manchester United. It was an emotional occasion in more ways than one because the recent announcement that rugby union was going professional sounded the death knell for Welsh players going north. All of us knew that sooner or later nearly all the team would be returning home for good. We had to make the most of what might turn out to be our last game together.

We gave England a good game but Martin Offiah was awarded two dodgy tries and we bowed out. I had the added disappointment of concussion after a collision with Dennis Betts' hipbone. A couple of weeks later Jonathan Davies returned to rugby union and over the course of the next year most of the rest of us followed. It is doubtful whether rugby league will ever again stage a successful world tournament. They simply don't have a world wide game and a World Cup will always be a three-horse race between Australia, New Zealand and England and the Aussies will nearly always win. An accident of history had served up a team of stars for Wales in 1995. Rugby league is club orientated and there is nothing wrong with that. What they should regret is the lost opportunity in South Wales to award a Super League franchise. Imagine what might have happened if that Wales team of 1995 had been thrown together as a club outfit a year earlier.

So there was much to ponder as the start of the 1999 World Cup drew nearer. I could sense the squad becoming nervous but the message from Graham was equally positive. 'You're as good as anyone,' he said, and we believed him.

The big day arrived at last and as we travelled through the streets of Cardiff to the Millennium Stadium the atmosphere was unreal. If I wasn't particularly nervous before, I certainly was now. Our routine in the changing-room was the same as always but we knew when we went out on to the pitch that this was a special match. The stadium had miraculously been completed in record time, but had we reached the starting line in tip-top condition?

Our opposition in that World Cup opener were Argentina. We had beaten them twice on their own patch three months before but on our big day we were less than convincing. We won but our performance disappointed us and Graham. Our families suffered more disappointment than most because they were unable to see either the opening ceremony or the game because the seats that they had been allocated were unfortunately behind the standing choir. Five days later we beat Japan easily and we knew we still needed to improve before our final pool match with Samoa. They had already lost to Argentina so we were a safe bet for a place in the quarter-finals whatever the result.

That was no consolation, however, after we had slumped to a careless defeat. We should have won. We had territorial advantage and set piece control for long periods – but our generosity with turnover ball was shocking. Pat Lam in the Samoan back row and Steve Bachop at fly-half had a field day and punished us for our many mistakes. I took exception to Lam's reported remarks at the end that 'Wales didn't respect us.' Nothing could have been further from the truth after his country had severely embarrassed Wales in the 1991 World Cup. In its own way this was an equally significant defeat because it brought to an abrupt and unexpected end our ten-match winning run and it also brought us down to earth. It was a timely reminder that we weren't the finished article – and awaiting us in the quarter-final were the pre-tournament favourites, Australia.

We knew that if we were to stretch the Wallabies we would have to be on top in the scrums and suck them in with our driving lineouts. We achieved parity in the first hour but the dominance never came. Neither did the tries against their brick wall defence. Instead, the referee did us no favours and awarded two of the most controversial tries you are ever likely to see. But we could not deny that Australia were the better team. It was no consolation that they returned to the Millennium Stadium a fortnight later to be crowned world champions.

We were defeated and deflated. Graham Henry was understandably disappointed. He was the product of a success culture and it was a difficult time. We didn't need to be told that we had failed to raise our game that vital extra 20 per cent but we broke up with Graham's words of thanks ringing in our ears. He told us that whatever we felt at that moment we shouldn't forget that we had regained a respect for Wales in world rugby. We had achieved something.

16

CAPTAINCY HAS A BLACK CLOUD

To be made captain of Wales in January 2000 was the greatest honour of my career. It was the culmination of everything I had striven for all my life. As I have said, when Graham Henry asked me to take over the leadership two months after the World Cup campaign, it was an offer I knew I had to accept not only for myself but for my parents, my sister Maria, April and the boys. There was that moment's hesitation when I considered the pros and cons but the answer had to be 'Yes'.

I had experienced the responsibility of captaincy enough times throughout my career to realise that the job didn't start and finish with 80 minutes of rugby. Graham had said that one of the factors in choosing me was the obvious respect I had from the rest of the squad and that was reassuring. It was the happiest squad I had ever been part of and to feel that I was an influential figure in it was a big boost. Little did I know that within a few weeks of taking over the leadership the make-up of the group, and to some extent its harmony, would be under serious threat from a totally unexpected source.

First there were a couple of bad results in the Six Nations matches. I have to admit that my first match as captain did not augur well as we lost heavily at home to France. Wales 3, France 36 was not the score-line I had hoped for. Suddenly all the public goodwill that had been built up over the previous 12 months seemed under threat. We had done well in the tight play, especially the scrums. I could take no personal pleasure from that. The French, as I had warned the team the night before, snapped up every loose ball – and there were several of them – and ran in three tries. Christophe Lamaison kicked 21 points.

The knives of the press boys were really out now. 'Dai-saster' and 'Shamed' were just two of the headlines in the Sunday papers. Welcome to the captaincy! I escaped the wrath of the more excitable accounts but, three months after he was the greatest thing since sliced bread, Graham Henry and the management team began to taste the more unpleasant side of the Welsh media. Match accounts are rarely straight down the middle when Wales have lost a rugby match. So the man who was once the Great Redeemer was now 'the world's highest-paid coach who will have his work cut out to explain the collapse'. You could almost sniff the changing mood in the air. I admitted afterwards that the result was a setback and we would hopefully learn from the experience. That might sound like an exercise in well-rehearsed platitudes but that was the situation we were in. I also said we would have to 'regroup', another cliché, but I couldn't in my wildest dreams have foreseen what was to happen next.

The 1999–2000 season saw Italy joining the other top European countries to form a new Six Nations Championship. To be absolutely frank that gave us a bit of a breathing space in our next match. Although they had, incredibly, beaten Scotland in their first match in Rome they were not expected to trouble us at the Millennium Stadium. Mercifully, they didn't. We won 47–16 and I had my first win under my belt as captain. Then it was England at Twickenham and the storm clouds were gathering. We knew that we would be underdogs. England were developing into an outstanding side and the pressure around us was greater than ever after some less than complimentary remarks about the team and in particular our fitness.

Bob Dwyer, my old mucker from the 1989 Lions' tour to Australia, was up and running again. The ex-Wallaby coach had made a good living from combining his coaching around the world – he had recently been with Leicester and was now with Bristol – with a high profile post as a media pundit. Before the French match he had given a television interview where he said that the Wales squad was not fit enough. Scott and Craig Quinnell had been particular targets for his comments when he said, 'There are too many guys carrying too much body fat. I think the Quinnells, for example, could be fantastically good rugby players. But there aren't many great fat players on the international circuit.'

When we had then lost so badly to France, Dwyer's criticism was given another airing and fuelled by further comments from the former England centre Jerry Guscott. He was in another television studio at the Millennium Stadium and concluded that against France we had played a good 40 minutes but had then, in his words, 'faded away'. His view was that our fitness and concentration had let us down and even when we beat Italy there was no escape from his criticism. This time it was a case of us not being able to finish the opposition off. If we had been fit, he claimed, we would have gone on to score 70 points.

So even as we prepared for Twickenham we knew the vultures were gathering. The message from Graham Henry and Steve Black had always been to expunge negative thoughts from our minds and we did our best. The team talked about victory and nothing else. On a personal note I had been suffering from backache during the week before the match. We started the game quite well but it was always a case of holding on rather than dominating proceedings. After about 15 minutes I was at a ruck when I felt a hefty blow to the small of my back. My back then went into muscle spasm and I could hardly move. I tried to run it off for about five minutes but if anything it got worse. There was no way I could go on and I had to come off. Graham asked Rob to assume the captain's duties for the second half. Rob was the obvious choice because he had captained Wales so many times previously. The rest of the game was hard to watch from the sidelines and in the second half England ran away with it. We weren't helped by a sin-binning that England exploited to the full by scoring 22 points. At the end of the game my back was so sore that I had to be helped into the bath and back out again. I was then helped to get dressed by Mike Wandsworth and taken back to the team hotel by the medical staff who refused to let me attend the after-match dinner. On the way to the dinner the management asked Rob to speak in my absence, Rob refused as he was obviously still hurting from losing the captaincy. To his great credit Garin Jenkins volunteered to speak on my behalf.

If we were disappointed in the immediate aftermath of the game it soon became very obvious that the rugby public were disenchanted. Some of the critics went in for the kill and some of them who were ex-internationals should have known better. They included people who had been invited by Graham Henry to be our mentors. I had taken that role to mean that they would give us moral support when things went wrong; positive advice and encouragement. Several of them did exactly that but how wrong could we have been about one or two others. Not for the first time J.J. Williams and Bobby Windsor were two of the worst culprits. 'JJ' had been part of the Welsh back-room staff himself for a short while in the 1980s but if I remember rightly his idea of fitness training amounted to little more than track running. His contribution didn't last long. I wonder what difference, in retrospect, he made to the teams of that period? I'll hazard a guess and say that he had a crack at it – and failed.

As for Bobby, people tell me that we shouldn't take him seriously.

Well, I can certainly vouch for that. I remember the time when Jonathan Humphreys, Andrew Lewis and I were invited to do a promotional shoot along with Graham Price, Charlie Faulkner and Bobby Windsor (the legendary Pontypool front row) and three young children, Thomas, Lewis and Owen. The promotion was to encourage youngsters to play in the front row, where the Union had identified a shortage. It was to be billed as 'The Past, The Present, The Future'. We all arrived at a given time at the National Sports Centre, Cardiff except Bobby who would not attend unless the Union paid him to do so. Bobby is always the first and harshest critic but it seems obvious that he is not prepared to give anything back to Welsh Rugby. He was a great hooker but I doubt whether his comments deserve any serious consideration these days.

Another source of criticism was from within Welsh rugby. If you accept that Graham Henry was not afraid to upset one or two people with his forthright views, you didn't have to be a genius to realise that there were people who would happily have seen the back of the upstart Kiwi. Successive generations of committees of enquiry have met, consulted and written reports all urging Welsh Rugby to start again with a blank sheet of paper. No one delighted in seeing Wales thrashed at Twickenham, but if the defeat led to the reining-in of the national coach, then it really would be a case of every cloud having a silver lining.

The main target of all the criticism became Steve Black. The fuss had started after Dwyer's comments in January. Blackie had tried to take the heat out of the situation with a tongue in cheek remark that if the Aussie felt that the Quinnell brothers were too fat and unfit he might like to come along and show them how to train properly. 'We would love to have the input of a coach of such great experience,' said Blackie. 'In fact he can have a training session with Craig if he likes, just to show Craig exactly what to do. I am sure that is something Craig would look forward to. Bob can even put on the impact pads for the session with Craig if he fancies that.' Bob Dwyer never took up the offer.

Unfortunately, the time for humour had long since gone after the England match. Something far more sinister was taking over. I have no doubt that there were people who saw the criticism of Blackie's fitness methods, matched against two bad defeats, as a stick to beat Henry with. If they thought they could destabilise the coach and the team by that route they were living in cloud cuckoo land. But the fate of Blackie was another matter.

There were people in the media who that month used methods that should cause them to hang their heads in shame when they look back in years to come. One man in particular – I suppose he would like to think of himself as an 'investigative journalist' – became very active in his enquiries in the north-east of England. That was Blackie's home territory but what this reporter hoped to find out by quizzing – or trying to quiz – the rugby and soccer players of Newcastle about their former fitness coach's methods remains an absolute mystery. My first thoughts were to confront the reporter but that would have given him importance beyond his worth.

The crux of the criticism aimed at Blackie revolved around the whys and wherefores of fitness tests. Alun Carter, the notational analyst for both Cardiff and Wales, put his finger on the nub of the issue. He said that the testing and monitoring of players was not a case of everyone being measured at one particular moment, it was, rather, continuous, accurate assessment. Every player needed an awareness of what he needed to do at any given time. Yet Blackie was not against testing. He fully intended to use it but he was sensitive enough to see that the players were worried – so he put the tests on hold.

Blackie's motto had always been one of 'Judge me by the results on the field.' For him it didn't matter one jot whether I was lifting five kilos more or running one second faster on the track. All of that would be totally irrelevant if Wales were losing matches. His methods, including his mind games, revolved around playing performance and for 18 months the players had been totally behind him. Others, apparently, were less enthusiastic, and a fortnight after the Twickenham debacle I suddenly realised that Blackie had decided that enough was enough.

There had been several casualties of the latest defeat, including Rob Howley and Chris Wyatt. On the eve of the Scottish match, I sat down with Blackie. I was still captain and my back injury had cleared up but all that paled into insignificance. Our chat began with his usual positive tone about how the squad had become his family and about how in a very short time the fate of the Wales team had become very important to him. Then came the bolt from the blue. His family, particularly his children, had become the targets for silly comments about his size, his methods and the failures of the Wales team. Also, he said, the criticism of himself was unfairly increasing pressure on Graham. So he had decided to go immediately after the following day's game with Scotland, win or lose.

I felt terrible. I knew there was little point in remonstrating with him. How could I when this wonderful family man had told me how his own loved ones were suffering? We both knew that he was only one-third of the way down the road we had set off on. He had certainly created an atmosphere and a sense of belonging that we all wanted to stay part of. He had set specific goals for individuals and they were committed to achieving them – for themselves and for Blackie. And he had consistently told us that we should settle for nothing less than being the best team in the world. And we believed him.

We talked for three hours. I knew he had made his decision but I simply didn't want to let go. If we kept on talking . . . well, perhaps it would never happen. Blackie and I had been particularly close. I owed him a lot. He had kept my career going. He had become a friend of April and the boys as well. But I knew that I had to respect his decision.

The following day we beat Scotland. Back in the dressing-rooms amongst all the celebrations I quickly noticed that Blackie was not around and asked Alan Lewis and JR, the kit man 'Where is Blackie?' I was told that Blackie was too emotional after the game and had decided to leave as quickly as he could. This immediately put a huge dampener on the celebrations. Showered and changed and on the way to the post-match functions the words on everyone's lips were 'Where's Blackie?' It was time to tell the rest of the team. This unhappy task was left to Dai Pickering. The disappointment and disbelief was clear to see and written all over the players' faces.

It was never in Blackie's nature to turn his back on friends and every one of us soon received a personal letter. To me he wrote, 'Your crazy sense of humour will be a particularly good memory from my time here. You're sharper than a really sharp thing that's gonna get sharper. Love, health and happiness to you, April and your lads, . . . God bless.'

It was an emotional time for us all. The press – and a few other people – had secured their pound of flesh. Early in the following week we were training again at the Welsh Institute of Sport. I was asked to give an interview for BBC Wales. There, on the microphone was that so-called investigative reporter who said, 'This must be a sad day for Wales?' I was almost speechless . . .

There was one more sting in the tail. An imperfect end to an unhappy month. We were still reeling from Blackie's departure and Graham Henry was genuinely upset but he had said nothing. Then 'Grannygate' landed on our laps. We had started our preparation for the final international of the campaign against Ireland when we noticed that Brett Sinkinson and Shane Howarth were absent. People don't believe us but the squad members, especially the senior players, rarely read the newspapers during international week. So we were a bit off the pace concerning the growing storm about the Welsh qualifications of two of the team.

Shane and Brett were now in the firing line and this was obviously a very serious matter. Graham Henry told us that both of them had decided to withdraw from the squad until the confusion was sorted out. But it never was. I had assumed, like everyone else, that they were both qualified. They were certainly model examples of commitment to the red shirt of Wales. After what had happened to Blackie only a few days before I began to think that I was in the middle of a recurring nightmare.

We had a senior players' meeting and Graham assured us again that everything would be resolved satisfactorily. I believed him. I had spoken to both Brett and Shane and knew them to be men of integrity. Yet the International Rugby Board ruled otherwise and they were forced to serve a period of residency. Personally I hope they will one day put on the red jersey again.

As Blackie had said, 'Where will this all end?'

17

FIT FOR THE LIONS

I almost never made the 2001 Lions tour to Australia – twice. In my own mind I had set out my stall about 18 months before. The frustrations of 1997 had made me more determined than ever to have achievable targets in the remaining years of my playing career. I wanted to make a success of the captaincy of Cardiff. I wanted to play in the World Cup for Wales. As the next Lions tour drew nearer, I realised that I also wanted to be a Lion for a third time.

It was my father who had predicted back in 1997 that I would tour in 2001. I thought he was crazy! I felt my form in the years since 1997 had justified my selection and made my Lions' ambitions realistic. I had held my place in the Wales team. At Graham Henry's insistence I took over as captain in January 2000 which had been a timely fillip. It was probably at that point that I decided to target the 2001 tour. Unfortunately a series of calf injuries were having a potentially disastrous effect on my ambitions.

I do not think that this book would be complete without a mention of my calves. For the last couple of years the name David Young and the word calves have in some people's eyes spelled trouble. The trouble that I have had has been well documented but only I and close friends know what my family has endured as a result of those blasted calves.

During the 1997–98 season I had started to have trouble with cramp and small muscle fibre tears. After particularly hard training sessions I suffered with severe cramps in both calves, the right worse than the left. After Christmas it became worse with cramps waking me at night. Because of the continuing cycle of muscle tear, after two weeks' rest from training I was examined by a doctor and told that it was possible that I was suffering from Compartment Syndrome.

I carried on playing at the request of the coaches until a few weeks before the end of the season but the length of time I played during each game became shorter and shorter. After the half-time break the calves would be very painful so eventually we decided that enough was enough and the problem had to be sorted before any serious damage was done.

I entered hospital for a simple operation on both calves to split the sheath around the muscle allowing the muscle more room. After two weeks I was able to resume light training again but not fast enough to make a tour to South Africa. The day we played the Australians in the quarter-final of the World Cup I remember setting myself for a scrum, and as we drove forward I felt a pain in my right leg that I likened to being shot. The pain was incredible and when Mark Davies, the physio, put his white towel over his shoulder I knew I was off. That evening was the worst I can remember and I was diagnosed with a very bad calf muscle tear. Considering past trouble with calves, I did wonder if I would recover sufficiently to play again. Recover I did and I thought that was the end to it.

Little did I know!

The cramps and tears started again towards the end of the 1999–2000 season and it was decided that another operation was needed. I hit what I think was the lowest point of my career. I had already missed the South Africa game because of a knee injury and I didn't want to miss any more. Family and friends rallied around to try and lift my spirits but having played international rugby for so long I began to wonder if my battered body was trying to tell me something.

After a weekend of thought, and lectures from my family that I still had much to offer, was I honestly prepared to give up my jersey so easy? The answer had to be NO. Definitely NO. I went ahead and had the operation only this time my recovery was not as simple.

During the next couple of weeks I was to be tested for a deep vein thrombosis and scanned, because there was a swelling under the scar which turned out to be old blood. After several days the scar opened and wept blood for a few weeks more. Then just as we thought it was healing nicely we noticed a ghastly smell, which April thought was dirty, smelly training kit in the boot of my car.

Four days before we were due to fly to Spain on our family holiday I was again admitted to hospital. The scar was reopened, cleaned out and plugged with antibiotic dressing to allow the now very large hole in my leg to heal from within. April and the boys travelled to Spain accompanied by my mother-in-law, Mair, without me yet again, as I was not allowed to fly. On her return April chauffeured me to the district nurse for almost ten weeks until eventually the scar healed. I was told on a visit to the specialist that I had been very lucky. The infection I had picked up somewhere along the line had started to eat away at the protective layer of fat around the muscle and another day or so and I would have been unable to play rugby for at least six months. But with all this behind me I could once again start rehabilitation. The new season was fast approaching and I was desperate to get fit and captain my club and country again. Throughout this period I received numerous supportive telephone calls from Graham Henry.

I worked hard during the coming weeks with Graham and Lynn Howells keeping in contact to see how I was progressing. At one point April noticed a local billboard with YOUNG ON WAY BACK on it. By the time I arrived home it was pinned to the fridge door just where I could see it. She is always very positive and will use any method. She and my parents kept reminding me that Cardiff had an important role to play in the Heineken Cup and there were autumn internationals to work for.

The club reached the start of the season raring to go although I had missed quite a bit of the pre-season training. I played those first couple of matches like they were my first ever but although not everything was 100 per cent perfect I was glad to be back on track.

I played the first few games. Then Disaster with a capital D. I had played barely ten minutes of the Edinburgh Reivers game when I set for a scrum. I knew straight away that all was not well. The right calf had gone again. I found out later that April had run to the tunnel after witnessing it from the stand and when she saw them bring me off she had burst into tears. Thankfully, my good friend Craig Quinnell had been there to take care of her. She knew better than most the hard work and sacrifices made by everyone during that summer to get me back on to that field and suddenly it all seemed for nothing. We were back to square one.

We left Cardiff Rugby Club before the game had ended. I had done everything that had been asked of me. I had undergone two operations on both legs, changed my weight training and running patterns and I had lost over 21lbs in body weight, all of which was to relieve the stress on my calves. I left Robert Norster and the staff in the medical room under no illusion that if something new could not be offered I would have no alternative but to retire. I was designed simply not prepared to put my family through this heartache every couple of weeks.

The following week I was a nightmare. April answered the phone – I was unable to speak to anyone. Clubmen, coaches, doctors and physios all phoned to tell me to stay positive. I was assured that rest was the answer and everything would work out. But how? I was not prepared to sit back for a couple of weeks, fight my way back to fitness only for the same thing to happen again. I knew deep down that I needed to see someone different. I do not mean at all to criticise the doctors I had already seen but it was obvious that there was an underlying problem and it would need a calf expert to sort it out. To their great credit Cardiff's back-room staff Jane James, Hywel Griffiths and Huw Wiltshire hunted tirelessly for the next few days until they came up with the name Mike Allen. He had been mentioned by several people outside Wales and in all honesty he was probably my last hope.

We travelled to Leicester to see Mike on Friday 8 September 2000 but I was definitely not prepared for his verdict on my very scarred legs. To my amazement he was totally shocked by what he saw. He said that he had never seen a right calf so swollen. After the examination he suggested that my problem was severe scarring around the Achilles tendon area which was not allowing the muscles to expand as they should. He likened it to glue over elastic bands. I was booked for a MRI scan that afternoon to confirm what he had diagnosed.

April, Hywel and I sat in a restaurant on the outskirts of Leicester and discussed the possible outcome. I can only say that it was good I was sitting down when Mike had given me the alternatives:

1. Rest, rehabilitation and resume playing but he admitted that there was a strong possibility that the calf would tear again.

2. An operation to clean the scar tissue away.

I was devastated, gobsmacked – I felt sick. Mike, seeing the shock on my face, advised me to return home to discuss the alternatives with April, my parents and respective coaches before making a decision.

It was agreed that there was no choice but to have the operation and I was booked in for two weeks' time. We travelled to Leicester and I had my operations. They were only supposed to take 45 minutes total but 2 hours 15 minutes later I still had not returned. April was worried sick. What had gone wrong? Mike entered my room as I was wheeled from recovery to tell April that I had just undergone major surgery to my right leg and that I would be unable to play for three months. My right calf had in effect exploded and was totally detached and in pieces inside my leg. Mike explained that he had sewn the muscle together and then reattached it but it would be a long road of recovery. I was still sedated and unaware of what was being said and by the time I recovered Mike and April had worked out a reasonable rehab programme that would hopefully see me fit to play England at the Millennium Stadium the following January.

Graham Henry was as positive as ever. He reassured me that the Wales captaincy was still mine when I regained full fitness. That was easier said than done but my will-power was as strong as ever. April urged me to be patient and not rush things but once I was back on my feet the hard work really started. Cardiff's conditioning expert, Huw Wiltshire, and the national squad's fitness coach, Peter Herbert, both played a vital part in my recovery. Wayne Mortimer worked tirelessly, giving me numerous massages often out of hours, and continues to do so.

Peter Herbert was developing a new fitness centre at the team's headquarters in the Vale of Glamorgan and his latest ingenious idea was something called a hypoxic chamber. This looked like a walk-in PVC tent but it was far more than that. Once inside it regulated the flow of oxygen with the aim of creating an atmosphere similar to that at 8,000 feet above sea level. As I grew stronger I then turned to the treadmill for running sessions of up to half-an-hour. By the end of November I felt confident enough to plan the games that would feature in my comeback. Cardiff had several matches in the lead-up to Christmas and the coach, Lynn Howells, agreed with me that I should start with 15 minutes in one game then a half hour in the next before a full match in early January. If everything went to plan I would be more than ready for the opening Six Nations match for Wales in February.

What did someone say about the 'best laid plans'? Seven days before Christmas I was finishing a training session with the Cardiff squad at UWIC. As I wiped some mud off my hand in the grass I felt a sudden burst of pain. I thought it was an electric shock from a live wire in the ground. No such luck. It was a piece of broken glass and with blood spurting everywhere I was taken to hospital for what I thought would be routine stitches. I was examined by hand specialist Dave Shearing, who informed me I had severed a nerve in my right hand. I was on my way back to theatre for another anaesthetic and more surgery. I was told that the injury would take a minimum of eight weeks to recover and I was definitely out of the England game. April drove down from Aberdare to meet me. It was hard not to believe that fate simply did not mean me to play in the internationals.

Yet again it was a case of coming to terms with the situation and setting another date for recovery. The imminent club matches were now out of the question. I was not exactly full of the joys of the festive season but the family were wonderfully supportive. Graham Henry insisted that with my hand stitched up and protected I could reasonably expect to play in Cardiff's cup match with local side, Bedwas, over the New Year weekend. I have to admit that I thought Graham was losing his marbles but the Great Redeemer is also the Great Persuader and, sure enough, two weeks later I was playing at last. It was only half a match and I was apprehensive about breaking the stitches. That would be catastrophic and would set me back another couple of months and leave my finger useless. At last, my luck had turned. I played the entire second half without mishap and, more importantly, I was back.

Before the end of January I came through three Heineken Cup matches. I cannot pretend that everything was sweetness and light because, blowing hot and cold, we played stunning rugby against Ulster at the Arms Park only to meekly go down in a sudden-death quarter-final at Gloucester. Wales fared little better in a heavy home defeat by England. After that there were better away performances against Scotland, France in Paris where we won again, and Italy. And as a season that for a long time threatened to pass me by drew to a close, I could again dream about resuming unfinished business with the British and Irish Lions.

18

LION-HEARTED TO THE END

The months of waiting and uncertainty came to an end on 25 April 2001. April and I had stayed in bed as late as possible. The British and Irish Lions' squad was to be announced at 11 a.m. on television. We wanted to make the time between as short as possible. I had met with Graham Henry to discuss my future. Everything looked rosy with Wales but he had also told me that my chance of a Lions' place was in the balance as the selectors were looking at John Hayes of Ireland. I was more than a little disappointed because although Hayes was six years younger, I felt I had more to offer. The decision was now out of my hands. I had done all I could with my performances in the Six Nations matches. I also felt that the Wales front five had outplayed every other front five, even England, in the tight but the final selection had come down to a Heineken Cup semi-final between Stade Francais and Munster. Several Irish players, including Hayes, had played but Munster had lost.

There had been an unsatisfactory end to the internationals when the tragic outbreak of foot-and-mouth disease had caused the postponement of three of Ireland's matches. The suggestion in many quarters was that the lack of rugby had put the Irish candidates at a disadvantage in the final Lions' selection. Maybe, maybe not. Some critics were brave enough to point out that although Ireland were on a roll with two wins, they had not been exposed to the might of England. Nor had they visited the Millennium Stadium to take on the Wales pack that had already had victories in Paris and Rome.

Whatever the permutations were for the selectors, I tried to block them out of my mind. That was not easy. Six months before, potentially worn out by five operations, the Lions' trip to Australia had seemed a tour too far . . . and here we were waiting for the squad to be announced.

I tried to keep myself busy and not think about the time. The children were playing upstairs and making too much noise as usual, while we tried to carry on as normal. When the clock ticked around to 10.30 I made a cup of tea and sat down to wait. The television pictures linked up with the press conference at the Crowne Plaza Hotel at Heathrow Airport. Syd Millar, a great prop himself who played tests for the Lions in New Zealand and South Africa and who went on to coach them to a famous win in 1974, was speaking about the past, present and future of the Lions. Then it was the turn of the 2001 manager, Donal Lenihan, to announce the squad.

Before he did so, he seemed to take an age thanking the advisors and his fellow-selectors for all their hard work. I just wanted him to get on with it. There had been no letter as in 1997. We had to wait for the list to be read out. I concentrated on the screen and listened as Lenihan named the players. April shouted, 'Yes, Yes!' and shook her fist in the air. I told her to shut up as my name had not been read out but she had seen something I had missed in my anxiety. The names were being rolled across the screen from right to left and mine had come into the graphics on the left side. April ran to the telephone to call my mother and all I could do was sit on the sofa and take in what was being said about the selections.

The kids came running down to find out what all the commotion was about. Thomas, being the oldest, got to the point: 'Is he going?' When April nodded he started to run around like a headless chicken. I still felt in a daze. I had tried desperately to hide my feelings from the family but I must confess I had been very nervous for several days and more than a little tetchy at times with the boys.

Now it was time for a family celebration. April confessed that she had decided against booking a restaurant the night before because she did not want to tempt fate. When we told the kids that we were eating out, we were given the usual response: 'But Dad, you know we have training at Abercynon tonight!' So the celebration ended up on the side of a very muddy rugby pitch in the rain as we watched the children train. Only they could have brought us down to earth at such a great speed.

Later, when the children were in bed, April and I sat down in front of the television. She was still smiling, and it was only then that what lay ahead really hit me. I was about to set off on my third Lions' tour. Most players would give their right arm to be on one so I had every right to enjoy the moment. One of the first reporters to congratulate me, Paul

Rees, pointed out that I would be the first Lion to play across three decades and in years to come I will remember that fact with pride.

As I continued to sit only half-watching the television my mind wandered back to 1997 when I had returned from South Africa very disappointed. My father, always the one to give the best advice at the right time, had said, 'Never mind – it's the Lions in 2001 for you, my boy.'

The Lions of 2001 finally assembled on 26 May at Tylney Hall, near Hook in Hampshire. We would have a week of kitting-out, training and getting to know one another and then, six days later, we would fly to Australia. Lady Luck, unfortunately, tried one more throw of the dice against me and, for nearly all that week of preparation, it looked as if I would not be heading east towards Heathrow Airport but in the opposite direction home to Aberdare.

As I had done 12 years before, I travelled to the pre-tour camp with the other Welsh players selected. This time there were ten of us, a good representation though this had already attracted criticism from some observers. I thought our selections were justified; in fact, a case could have been made for even more, especially Scott Gibbs. The first laugh of the week was when we arrived by mini-bus and several English players arrived in their BMWs and Mercedes. Nothing changes!

The laughing stopped for me the very next morning. I had picked up a calf strain the week before when Wales had played an end-of-season match against the Barbarians. Not so long ago, if you were picked for a Lions' tour you did not play again after Easter. Players like Phil Bennett were even forced to miss cup finals because of that. These days we play on to the bitter end.

I don't think Graham Henry was overjoyed about the game, but he remained positive in public. Privately, he told the Lions that they would not play the whole 80 minutes. He didn't want any of us injured or exhausted with the tour so near. Graham hadn't bargained for Young's Curse. Two minutes before half-time I felt a twinge in my right calf but was not unduly worried about it although I sat out the second half. I had vowed to be in peak condition for the tour and, ever since my selection, had been sprinting on the local fields. A few days after the Barbarian game, foolishly as things turned out, I resumed this lonely regime. I was on the sixth of the ten 220-yard runs I had set myself when I felt the calf muscle tighten again. Time to stop and put an ice pack on the leg.

Before I left for Tylney Hall the Cardiff physiotherapist, Jayne James, had examined the leg, said it should be fine and I had thought no more of it. Then, on that first morning's Lions' training, the sharp pain returned. Panic set in. Fortunately, there were several people on the back-room staff who knew me well. Steve Black had been re-united with Graham Henry and the Wales team physiotherapist, Mark Davies, was also there again. His diagnosis was that the muscle was obviously sore and needed further rest. But time was not on my side. The Lions were leaving in five days and there was only one other tight-head prop, England's Phil Vickery, in the squad.

Graham and Donal Lenihan spoke to me almost immediately and said they would probably need to make a decision about my further involvement on the Monday morning. The alarm bells were now ringing with a vengeance. One of the great things about the Lions of 2001 was that Graham had wisely assembled an experienced coaching and management team around him. As well as Mark Davies and the masseur Richard Wegrzyk, another link with 1997 was the team doctor James Robson. He is a wonderfully calming influence. When he examined me the following day he could see that I was worried. 'You've torn some fibres,' he said, 'but this is a different injury from the ones you've had before.' That was the good news. The bad was that I might need two to three weeks to fully recover and the management would not wait that long. I insisted that on past experience I knew I would be all right after a week. Donal was sympathetic but said that he would have to discuss the situation with Graham and James. At that point I thought my tour might be over before it had begun and rang April to tell her. She told me to snap out of it!

There was a slight improvement by the following day and Donal Lenihan gave me the benefit of the doubt. 'We'll give you a week,' he said, 'but you must train next Tuesday in Perth or we will be forced to send for someone else.' I was grateful for that but for the next two or three days there was no further improvement. I remained positive and was even more determined to pull through after a conversation with Lawrence Dallaglio. We were dining together at Tylney Hall when he came out with the amazing revelation that he was not fit for contact training and he wouldn't be ready to play for three weeks. I knew that he was struggling with a knee injury picked up playing for Wasps but until then hadn't realised the extent of it. It was a bit of a bombshell because what it effectively meant was that whereas I had to be fit inside a week Lawrence had the luxury of another fortnight before he was expected to play. Allowing for the fact that there were only two tight-heads but the back row could be shuffled with several permutations, it still didn't strike me as particularly fair. What made matters even worse was that the inside-centre, Mike Catt, was struggling with back and calf injuries and he, too, had been told to get himself fit for later in the tour.

There was, of course, one essential difference between Catty, Lawrence and me: they seemingly had been pencilled in for the provisional test XV and I wasn't. That was a situation I would come to terms with as the tour progressed but for the time being I could only concentrate on my fitness.

My luck changed when we reached Perth. Mark Davies had treated me three or four times a day and Blackie picked up where he had left off with me in the Wales squad over a year before. Everything he said encouraged me to keep at it and by the following Monday I was ready to work on the weights in the gym and run on the treadmill. On the next day I completed two-thirds of a full training session. I would have done more but James Robson stopped me and said, 'You've done enough – you're well on track to play next week.' My day was complete when Graham and Donal also congratulated me.

During a conversation with April that evening she told me that Mike Allen had contacted her after reading an article in the paper. He wanted to reassure me that as far as he was concerned there could be no serious problem with the calf, because anything which could have caused a problem had been removed during my recent operation. He was adamant that with regular stretching and some rest I would be fine.

Something else had driven me on ever since we had assembled at Tylney Hall. The management had shared with us the two provisional line-ups for the opening games in Australia. I was due to play in the second game – and I was to be captain. To miss the tour after being on the verge of such an honour would have been a sickening blow, so when the all-clear was finally given I sat back and let it all sink in. I had told April of their intentions when I first phoned home and that made her doubly determined to gee me up. Her encouragement, as always, had helped me pull through a crisis.

Now I could enjoy another accolade for myself, and the family. I watched from the stand as the Lions scored over 100 points in the tour-opener against Western Australia and then we flew across to Townsville for the second game and my great moment. Our opponents were to be the Queensland President's XV and as captain for the day I sat alongside

Graham and Donal for the team announcement. A comparatively minor episode at the press conference reminded me again of the occasional tardiness of the Welsh media compared to their counterparts elsewhere.

When the formal part of the press conference had finished several London-based journalists warmly congratulated me on the captaincy. They included people who had written profiles on me over the preceding months and remembered the injuries I had overcome to be on the tour in the first place. There was however a totally different response from BBC Wales. I was interviewed for radio by Huw Llywelyn Davies and his first words were, 'Congratulations, but you must be disappointed because being mid-week captain aren't you unlikely to be in the test side?' That was the typically negative approach I had come to expect from my fellow countrymen. Here was I, the first Welshman to lead a Lions' side since Jeff Squire in 1983, and all he could do was start with something like that. I pointed out to him that we were only talking about the second match of the tour, that the test side was something for another day and that for the time being I was immensely proud to be the leader of any Lions' combination.

As for the game itself, I was apprehensive about the team talk beforehand because of the quality of players named in the team, a few of whom had already captained their country, but once I had started it all seemed to come quite naturally. I told the players that we had a hard act to follow after the 116–0 scoreline at Perth and that although our opposition was much tougher we had to keep the ball rolling. In time-honoured fashion I led the team out and happily scored the first try in the tenth minute. It was the well-rehearsed catch-and-drive move from a lineout on the left and I was carrying the ball as the rest of the pack drove me over and down. My luck was really changing for the better!

We struggled until half-time when the score was only 10–6 in our favour but in the next 40 minutes ran freely to tot up another 73 points without reply. At the end I thought we had done a good job. I had the personal bonus of no injury worries. The calf was a bit stiff the next day but that was nothing untoward. Less encouraging was the fact that only four of our starting line-up were named in the team for the first big Saturday game of the tour against Queensland Reds. The evidence was mounting that the test side had been picked before we left home. Injuries which go hand-in-hand with any Lions' tour would, however, inevitably force a change of tack in some positions – the young Scottish number 8 Simon Taylor was already on the way home and Phil Greening looked set to follow him – but Phil Vickery was clearly destined for the tight-head prop spot. The team played well for 40 minutes against the Reds and all I could do was wait for another chance in the next mid-week game against Australia A. That was to go badly wrong.

One of the problems of the itinerary that had quickly became obvious was that by travelling every Sunday – and in Australia that usually meant by air over considerable distances – and by playing every Tuesday the mid-week side would only ever have one day's preparation, on the Monday. That was far from ideal and it backfired badly on us against Australia A. Our lack of practice haunted us in the lineouts where we lost as many as nine on our own throw-in. That was totally unacceptable. Sensing that we were struggling in that department the Aussies had challenged us at every throw.

We also had problems in other aspects of the game. In the lead-up there had been an orchestrated campaign in the local press against our alleged illegal tactics at rucks and mauls and that had made us wonder if we were being over-vigorous. That was no good against a side that were undoubtedly good at snapping up loose ball on the ground. We were penalised to the tune of 24 penalties, a few of which were given against our scrum when it was clear that we were definitely on top in that area. We studied the match video later, and we couldn't for the life of us work out what we were doing wrong.

Due to the high penalty count against us we never gained any field position nor could we gain any momentum but worst of all were our lineout problems. Unfortunately we were never likely to be in a position to win the game, but we did manage to score a couple of late tries which showed what we could have achieved if we had had possession in the right areas of the field. In the end the score read 25–28. To complete our misery Mike Catt had broken down before half-time with a recurrence of his calf injury and was out of the tour, and late in the game Lawrence Dallaglio was sin-binned for persistent infringement. Though we didn't realise it at the time, his tour would also be over by the end of the week.

The reception afterwards was short and there was no mixing between the two sides. I was disappointed for the team because they had paid the ultimate price largely through no fault of theirs. I knew that privately they would be thinking like me that a place in the test team in ten days' time was now out of reach.

What we could not have anticipated was that Graham would go public about a change of priorities on their part. No coach likes to see his team lose but it was obvious that Graham was less than pleased with our performance. His response at the press conference was surprising in its simplicity. Graham mentioned that a contributory factor to the loss was that the team had been able to have only one training session together because of the tour schedule. The press asked the question 'How could that change for the following mid-week games?' Graham's only answer could be that we would need to concentrate on the Saturday games and get through the mid-week games as best we could. I knew what Graham was trying to say but it was difficult to put it across. The press being the press tried to make more than there really was and could not wait to tell as many mid-week players as possible, hoping for a really juicy reaction.

We faced a long week ahead before our next opportunity to play and an even longer three weeks after that when there would be only one more mid-week game. This was not the ideal scenario for anyone, and I was already thinking about my approach with the team when most of us next played against New South Wales Country – but a lot of water flowed under the bridge before then.

First up was the Waratahs at Sydney Football Stadium and that turned into a blood-bath. The team was playing really well and we were 20 points up at half-time but the home side were very physical and the team we had put out were not prepared to take a step back. The Waratahs' fly-half, Duncan McRae, was correctly sent off for assaulting – there can be no other word for it – Ronan O'Gara with 11 punches. Five other players, two of them Lions, were sin-binned. The first yellow card had been waved against one of their locks right at the kick-off. It was that sort of match.

Bob Dwyer, who was now coach of the home side, told a live television audience that the fault lay with Graham Henry and the Lions. To everyone's astonishment he said, 'He comes from New Zealand and Kiwis never take responsibility for any problems in a game.' For his part, Graham said it was a 'black day for rugby'. No one could seriously disagree. If there was any credit to be gained from such a game it was that the Lions had shown self-discipline against a team that was clearly set on pre-meditated violence. Donal Lenihan was angrier than most and said the only comparison that sprang to mind was what had happened to the Lions of 1971 when, a week before the first Test, a vicious assault by the Canterbury pack had resulted in both first-choice props being ruled out of the tour.

All the unpleasantness surrounding the Waratahs' match was soon put into perspective with the news of the tragic death of our baggage-man,

Anton Toia. He had worked all hours throughout the tour attending to our every need, with laundry and kit bags and anything you cared to mention. We were at Coffs Harbour preparing for the NSW Country match when several of the team came into the hotel and shouted, 'Anton's drowned!' We couldn't believe it because Anton was a strong swimmer, but after a spot of whale-watching with a few of the boys, he had opted to swim back to shore. He never made it, suffering a heart attack in the water.

My pre-match captain's meeting was scheduled for later that evening. I cancelled it. Suddenly rugby didn't seem that important.

There was one happier event in that dire week. Mike Catt's unfortunate injury had resulted in an SOS to Scott Gibbs to join us. Gibbsy arrived in typical fashion. We were having a rare evening out in Doyle's Seafood Restaurant overlooking Sydney Harbour when in walked the pocket battleship, a huge smile on his face, to shake everyone's hand and say, 'Hello.' The buzz he created was impressive, to say the least. I know I'm biased but as far as I was concerned Gibbsy should have been an automatic choice when the squad was first selected. Somehow, we all knew that sooner or later he would turn up in Australia and now the tour party was stronger for his presence. I looked forward to him playing in the side against the Country XV.

My message in the changing-room at Coffs Harbour was quite simple: 'It's your last chance to stake a claim but we must remember that we are a team. We must go into the game collectively and stick to the game plan. We mustn't fall back again on the excuse of not enough preparation time – we are international players.' Deep down I think all of us knew that at that stage of the tour it was more a case of the Saturday players playing themselves out of test contention rather than the rest of us playing ourselves in. However we got back to our winning ways. Scott Gibbs, as expected, brought more power to mid-field and though it was by no means a great team performance we managed six tries and 46 points – and I was on the score sheet again!

I didn't expect to be named in the first Test side and I also knew that if we went one up in the series any future test chance was unlikely. Like everyone else in the squad, however, I desperately wanted us to win. What happened at The Gabba in Brisbane is already part of rugby folklore. The 29–13 victory was a brilliant team performance and it was rightly a cause for mass celebration by the team and the hordes of travelling supporters. I caught a bit of flak afterwards for saying that although I was delighted with victory in Brisbane, I felt like an outsider and it was not mine to celebrate. I had watched from the stand and I am not a great watcher. Not long after we left the stadium I was heading for bed to catch up with my beauty sleep.

Before I did though I was consulted on an issue that was threatening to tarnish the test victory. The Northampton scrum-half Matt Dawson had written a newspaper article which contained several direct criticisms of the Lions' management. Amongst other things he had complained about what he called 'mindless training' and the fact that 'GH doesn't inspire me at all . . . too much shouting and screaming'. What was doubly unfortunate was that the article had appeared in the UK hours before the first Test kicked off. I couldn't agree with his reported remarks that there was discontent in our ranks. We sat together in the team room.

'Have you heard about the article?' he asked. I said that I had and he admitted that it had all gone horribly wrong. I couldn't disagree but told him that he had to face up to the problem and work out what he was going to do about it the next morning. Eventually we spoke again after breakfast and then he talked to the players. He admitted, to his credit, that he had written the article himself and that it was his sole responsibility. He could only apologise to everyone and said he would take any punishment that was coming his way. He also promised to make it up to everyone in his next match. I admired him for standing up to tell us all this – and 48 hours later the incident had a happy ending when he played a blinder against the ACT Brumbies and slotted the match-winning conversion in injury time. No sooner had he done so than he pointed theatrically to the Lions' crest on his shirt and mouthed to one and all in the stands, 'I'm a Lion!' The majority of us had never doubted that.

The fall-out from Daws' article continued for a bit longer. Clearly there were issues he had raised that had to be discussed. Were we split? Were too many of us being ignored? Was the tour boring?

Donal Lenihan wisely called a senior players' meeting. With me in the group were Lawrence Dallaglio, Keith Wood and the captain, Martin Johnson. We were asked a straightforward question: 'Is there a rift between players and management?'

I told them that there were no gripes from the mid-week team other than an understandable concern about a lack of real opportunities to win selection for the big matches – and that, in turn, could be traced back to the lack of proper preparation for our own matches. The basic problem was that all the emphasis was on preparing a strong team for the Saturday matches. They accepted what I said – but could not see a way around the problem.

There was a danger that in all the soul-searching about Daws' comments we were forgetting the great victory in the first Test. One final demon had to be exorcised. There was widespread speculation in the press that he would be sent home as a disciplinary measure. Thankfully, the management rejected such a knee-jerk reaction and we headed for Canberra for the final mid-week game of the tour.

Once again I had to rack my brain for a new approach at the pre-match captain's meeting. I was also still annoyed about a press conference on the Monday when the press had tried to compare us with the notably unsuccessful 1993 'dirt-trackers'. Too many of that team apparently had gone missing in action and by the end of their tour they were thoroughly discredited. I resented any such comparison and told the press as much. The Lions of 2001, all of them, had worked hard from first to last.

So to the captain's meeting and I eventually came up with something different. A media guide had been produced in which, amongst other things, all the players had said what being a Lion meant to them. This provided me with all the ammunition I needed. I went around the room reading out the answers given by every player there. They hardly differed from one another: 'It's a lifetime dream' (Balshaw); 'The top honour one can achieve in British and Irish rugby' (Cohen); 'The pinnacle of the career of any British and Irish rugby player' (Davidson); 'Everything' (Healey); 'A dream come true' (Morris); 'It's the fulfilment of a lifetime's ambition' (Mark Taylor); and so on, through every one of the 22 players in the room.

It only remained for me to remind them that we were at the crossroads. Did we really want to finish our personal contributions to the squad of 2001 with another defeat? Or did we want to go home with our heads held high?

I felt sure that mentally the team was prepared to take on the Brumbies at the magnificent Bruce Stadium. At half-time I began to wonder if I was kidding myself. We were 10–22 down and only hanging on thanks to an interception try by Austin Healey. We had real problems. Back in the changing-room I appealed, 'Have we forgotten everything we said last night?' We needed to play a pick up and go game and get behind them. 'This is our big game,' I said. 'Let's go out there and do it!' We had one big team squeeze and went back on to the pitch knowing we needed to score first. We did. And at the very end, with the hooter for full-time already having sounded, we kept the ball alive through a dozen phases and Austin Healey scored the equalising try half-way out on the left. And Dawson converted. The players had shown to everybody the character, team spirit and togetherness that I had been talking about for weeks. I felt that this win was totally what they deserved. Our tour could have ended there.

It didn't, of course. There were ten days and two tests to come – and what happened during them changed the perceptions of the 2001 Lions completely. For a start we lost both tests and the series. After the first of them, at the Colonial Stadium in Melbourne, I began to wonder whether I would get a test match under my belt after all. Against all predictions our scrum had struggled. Some of the press had suggested that I should be brought in to add some extra scrummaging power as in their opinion Phil Vickery had not been a dominating force at tight-head. I thought I might have a chance for the third Test and was disappointed when no one spoke to me. Wasn't I in contention at all? I went to see the forwards' coach, Andy Robinson.

'Andy,' I said, 'I thought I might be in with a chance for the third Test but could you explain to me where I have lost out on selection?' He pointed out that in the selectors' opinion Vickery's defence was better and he carried the ball more. I could only reply that the statistics for the tour showed that we had both topped the front row tackle count twice so there was no significant difference. They also showed that I had carried the ball more times than him. I accepted that Vickery's Six Nations performances in both areas had been impressive but on tour we were neck and neck.

Although I was disappointed not to be given a chance I was always 100 per cent behind Vickery. Andy went on to say that he had spoken to Vickery about his performance in the second Test and he would play again in the third at Sydney. He had a role for me, however. He wanted me to spend time with Vickery working on his body angles in the scrum and to also work with the test front row as a unit. I suppose it was a compliment of sorts.

We lost that final test and even as we came to terms with our disappointment one more self-inflicted storm broke over our heads. Austin Healey had gone one better than Matt Dawson in the London papers a fortnight before. Where Daws had criticised his own colleagues Austin had decided to have a go at the Aussie male in general and one of his opponents, Justin Harrison, in particular. That was just what we didn't need on the final weekend of the tour.

Only Austin, all five-foot nine of him, could stoke up a feud with a six-foot eight lock-forward. It had been developing nicely for several weeks. In the Australia A game Harrison had stamped on Will Greenwood and Austin, never slow in coming forward, gave him a clip and a bit of verbal. They exchanged further pleasantries in the Brumbies' game in Canberra and, at the very end, Harrison kneed Austin after he had scored his last-gasp try. Ironically, the dead leg that came from that eventually threatened Austin's hard-won test place.

But before he was forced to withdraw from the final test at Sydney, with a back spasm, he had gone ahead with his pop at Harrison in the paper. No one was amused, least of all the management. We had been told all along not to give ammunition to the opposition that could be thrown back in our faces. Austin Healey was very much in the wrong. But it was difficult to be too angry with him.

I'll say it straight out: I like Austin Healey. I liked him before and, though for a moment several of us would happily have throttled him, I like him now. I get on well with him because he's a real character. Yes, he says things without thinking and, yes, this particular attempt to be funny backfired badly. But the suggestion that his article cost the Lions the series is absolute rubbish.

The morning after the final test I felt for Graham. There were people against him before he had even set out. I well remember several dinners during the Six Nations season when committee-men had questioned me about the wisdom of his appointment as coach – but only on the grounds that he 'wasn't British'.

He knew that the eyes of the doubters had been on him for months but it wasn't because of them that he was so disappointed with the final outcome. He wanted success for the sake of the team. To achieve it he had meticulously assembled a good back-up team around him, and he and they had worked incredibly hard. He had been rigorous in his pre-tour analysis of what was needed to succeed. I had said before the tour and I say it again – Graham is by far the best coach in Britain and nothing that happened on the tour changed my mind. He thoroughly deserved the appointment of head coach to the Lions, but somewhere along the line all the parts didn't quite gel. His defence coach Phil Larder made no secret of the fact, for instance, that he needed to work harder with the Celts than with the English players in his charge. That was a perfectly fair assessment and I am the first to admit that we have fallen behind England, even though it gives me little pleasure to say so.

Even before the Lions left Sydney there were unhealthy signs that some people would not allow the dust to settle on the 2001 tour. So-and-so would, we were told, sooner or later say this; and another so-and-so would also join in and say that. I was even targeted by some sensation seekers who speculated that I would confront Graham about the demoralised group of Welsh players on tour. They didn't know me.

What we say to the players who didn't go to Australia is that we were the lucky ones. The ones who had a burning ambition to become a Lion and who achieved it. That is what we will look back on in years to come – and we will do so with a special pride.

In my case it will be strengthened by the knowledge that a sporting life that started in Penywaun and was supported by a magnificent family took me to the captaincy of Salford, Cardiff, Wales and the British Lions. A career spanning three decades.

That can't be bad.

Statistics

David Young's Career Record (as at 31 July 2001)

RUGBY UNION

INTERNATIONALS FOR WALES

1987

England	Brisbane	World Cup	W	16–3
New Zealand	Brisbane	World Cup	L	6–49
USA	Cardiff		W	46–0

1988

England	Twickenham	W	11–3
Scotland	Cardiff	W	25–20
Ireland	Dublin	W	12–9
France	Cardiff	L	9–10
New Zealand	Christchurch	L	3–52
New Zealand	Auckland	L	9–54
Western Samoa	Cardiff	W	28–6
Romania	Cardiff	L	9–15

1989

Scotland	Murrayfield	L	7–23
New Zealand	Cardiff	L	9–34

1990

France	Cardiff	L	19–29

1996

Australia	Cardiff	L	19–28
South Africa	Cardiff	L	20–37

1997

USA	Cardiff	W	34–14
Scotland	Murrayfield	W	34–19
Ireland	Cardiff	L	25–26
France	Paris	L	22–27
England	Cardiff	L	13–34
Romania	Wrexham	W	70–21
New Zealand	Wembley	L	7–42

1998

Italy	Llanelli	W	23–20
England	Twickeham	L	26–60
Scotland	Wembley	W	19–13
Ireland	Dublin	W	30–21
France	Wembley	L	0–51

1999

Ireland	Wembley		L	23–29
England (rep)	Wembley		W	32–31
Argentina (rep)	Buenos Aires		W	36–26
Argentina (rep)	Buenos Aires		W	23–16
South Africa	Cardiff		W	29–19
Canada (rep)	Cardiff		W	33–19
France	Cardiff		W	34–23
Argentina	Cardiff	World Cup	W	23–18
Japan	Cardiff	World Cup	W	64–18
Samoa	Cardiff	World Cup	L	31–38
Australia	Cardiff	World Cup	L	9–24

2000

France	Cardiff	(Captain)	L	3–36
Italy	Cardiff	(Captain)	W	47–16
England	Twickenham	(Captain)	L	12–46
Scotland	Cardiff	(Captain)	W	26–18
Ireland	Dublin	(Captain)	W	23–19

2001

England	Cardiff	(Captain)	L	15–44
Scotland	Murrayfield	(Captain)	D	28–28
France	Paris	(Captain)	W	43–35
Italy	Rome	(Captain)	W	33–23

Total internationals: 48
Record as captain: Played 9 Won 5 Lost 3 Drawn 1

OTHER GAMES FOR WALES XV

1999

Tucuman	Tucuman	W	69–44
Argentina A	Rosario	L	34–47

2001

Barbarians	Cardiff	(Captain)	L	38–40

FOR THE BRITISH LIONS

TESTS

1989

Australia	Sydney	L	12–30
Australia	Brisbane	W	19–12
Australia	Sydney	W	19–18

OTHER GAMES

1989

Western Australia	Perth	W	44–0
Queensland	Brisbane	W	19–15
New South Wales	Sydney	W	23–21
Australian Capital Territory (rep)	Canberra	W	41–25
ANZAC XV	Brisbane	W	19–15

1997

Border	East London	W	18–14
Mpumalanga (rep)	Witbank	W	64–14
Northern Transvaal (rep)	Pretoria	L	30–35
Natal	Durban	W	42–12
Free State	Bloemfontein	W	52–30
Northern Free State	Welkom	W	67–39

2001

Queensland President's XV	Townsville	(Captain)	W	83–6
Australia A	Gosford	(Captain)	L	25–28
New South Wales Country	Coffs Habour	(Captain)	W	30–28
ACT Brumbies	Canberra	(Captain)	W	30–28

FOR THE BARBARIANS

1987

Newport	Newport	W	44–28

1988

East Midlands	Northampton	W	52–13
Cardiff	Cardiff	W	32–27
Australia	Cardiff	L	22–40

1989

New Zealand	Twickenham	L	10–21

CLUB RUGBY APPEARANCES

1985–86	Neath	1
	Swansea	3
1986–87	Swansea	19
1987–88	Swansea	20
1988–89	Cardiff	17
1989–90	Cardiff	16
1996–97	Cardiff	16

1997–98	Cardiff	20	
1998–99	Cardiff	18	(Captain)
1999–00	Cardiff	10	(Captain)
2000–01	Cardiff	13	(Captain)

RUGBY LEAGUE

INTERNATIONALS FOR WALES

1991

Papua New Guinea		Swansea		W	68–0

1992

France	Swansea		W	35–6
England	Swansea	(Captain)	L	11–36
France	Perpignan	(Captain)	W	19–18

1993

New Zealand	Swansea		L	19–24

1994

France	Cardiff		W	13–12
Australia	Cardiff	(Captain)	L	4–46

1995

England	Cardiff		W	18–16
France	Carcassone		W	22–10
France	Cardiff	World Cup	W	28–6
Western Samoa	Swansea	World Cup	L	22–10
England	Manchester	World Cup	L	10–25

1996

France	Carcassone	(Captain)	W	34–14

Total internationals: 13
Record as captain: Played 4 Won 2 Lost 2

CLUB RUGBY APPEARANCES

1989–90	Leeds	3	
1990–91	Leeds	5	
1991–92	Salford	29	
1992–93	Salford	29	(Captain)
1993–94	Salford	33	(Captain)
1994–95	Salford	34	(Captain)
1995–96	Salford	21	(Captain)
1996	Salford	7	Super League